THE
BAKER STREET IRREGULAR

THE UNAUTHORISED BIOGRAPHY OF SHERLOCK HOLMES

Mr Sherlock Holmes of Baker Street.
Possibly the only extant photograph of the famous detective.
Taken around 1887.

THE
BAKER STREET IRREGULAR

THE UNAUTHORISED BIOGRAPHY OF SHERLOCK HOLMES

AUSTIN MITCHELSON

IAN HENRY PUBLICATIONS
PLAYERS PRESS

© Austin Mitchelson, 1994

0 86025 461 5

Published simultaneously in the U.K. and the U.S.A. by
Ian Henry Publications, Ltd.
20 Park Drive, Romford, Essex RM1 4LH
and
Players Press, Inc.
P O Box 1132, Studio City, California 91614-0132

Printed in England
and Produced by
Ennisfield Print & Design
London E1

THIS IS FOR TOM

"The world is full of obvious things which nobody by any chance ever observes." - *Sherlock Holmes*

Contents

Introduction

Chronology

A Scandal in Baker Street

A Study in Childhood

A Case of Ambition

The Irregular Band

The Seeds of Failure

The Crooked Professor

The Curious Incident of Sherlock Holmes and the Whitechapel Murders

The Exceptional Policeman

A Murder in Cold Blood

The Authorised Version

The Second victim

The Official Agent

The Unscrupulous Accessory

The Final Moves

Bibliography

Appendix: The Crimes of Sherlock Holmes

INTRODUCTION

Doctor John Watson once remarked that Sherlock Holmes was the 'best and wisest' man he ever knew. It was a naïve and inaccurate verdict. For Holmes was an unprincipled, ruthless opportunist who used the weakness and vulnerability of others to further his own financial ends.

Curiously, although the Doctor was prone to making plauditory statements such as that, he did not attempt in his records of Holmes's cases to conceal the true nature of the detective. The addiction to cocaine and morphine is openly discussed and in the course of various exploits, Watson reported how murderers were allowed to go free, conspiracies were entered into, evidence was deliberately destroyed, burglaries were committed and illegal searches were made.

Somehow, the impression is given that such illegal acts serve the interests of justice and that Sherlock Holmes was, as he said himself, 'the last and highest court of appeal'. There was, however, a marked divide between what Holmes said and what he did. He claimed, for example, that his fees were on a fixed scale which he did not vary 'save when I remit them altogether'. In fact, he charged widely varying sums, apparently basing his demands on the wealth of the client and the degree of anxiety he or she was suffering.

Watson did not comment on these apparent discrepancies; he was content to report the facts and allow the reader to judge. Unfortunately, our judgement has been clouded by an industry which has grown up around the image of Sherlock Holmes; the Holmes of the movies, the stage, television, radio and comic books, is not the Holmes whose exploits were recorded by Dr. Watson. He has become a mythological figure, an icon of Victorian England, taking a place alongside cheerful cockney urchins, beautiful young flower sellers, roast chestnuts, kind-hearted benefactors, and thick London fog. The reality was very different; it was a time of violence, cruelty, grinding poverty and child prostitution.

His career as a private inquiry agent began in 1875 and ended in 1903. His activities were recorded by Dr. Watson and it is his fifty-six short stories and four novels which are our prime source of evidence. Occasionally we must look elsewhere, for Watson was unaware of some matters or failed to detail them, but it is the writings of the doctor which provide the basis and corroboration for most of the conclusions reached here.

Sherlock Holmes decided early in his career that it was the rich and powerful who, if they could be persuaded to use his services, would make him a wealthy and successful man. As a result he took active measures to ensure that he was socially acceptable and available. He would go to whatever lengths were necessary to resolve his wealthy clients' problems in return for their gratitude and a substantial fee. His readiness to step outside the law is clear from the catalogue of blackmail, fraud, burglary, suppression of material evidence, conspiracy to pervert the course of justice and accessory to murder, that we find in Dr. Watson's records. Additionally there is conclusive evidence of at least seven cold-blooded murders by Sherlock Holmes.

Almost as alarming as his illegal activities was his apparent incompetence as an inquiry agent. At least one client lost his life because of Holmes's negligence, a kidnap victim died when Holmes failed to act in time and there were numerous terrifyingly narrow escapes for people who had placed their trust in him. It is clear from Watson that Holmes would, while under the influence of drugs, consult with and act for his clients. It may have been this addiction which had a seriously debilitating effect on his performance.

A critical and careful study of the cases recorded by Dr. Watson shows Sherlock Holmes to be far from the cool, even-handed Victorian gentleman-adventurer that we have come to believe. It has also revealed for the first time the truth about Holmes's part in the death of Professor James Moriarty; the rôle played in the Jack the Ripper murders in London's East End, how a card game led to the death of an innocent man at the hands of Sherlock Holmes, why, in 1897, two doctors and Holmes's next of kin assembled at 221B Baker Street and the reason that Sherlock Holmes's career came to an abrupt and final end in 1903.

CHRONOLOGY

There has always been a degree of uncertainty about the dating of the events in Sherlock Holmes's life. Dr. Watson's memory, when he came to set down details of the cases, was far from infallible and scholars have done much work on establishing a definitive chronological order of Holmes's exploits.

Much of the mystery was dispelled in 1955 when the late William Baring-Gould published his meticulous research and his dating of the cases has achieved wide acceptance. Consequently, I have confidently adopted his conclusions for the purpose of this assessment of the life and work of Sherlock Holmes.

Dr John H Watson. A photograph taken prior to his embarkation for Afghanistan.

CHAPTER ONE

A Scandal in Baker Street

Doctor Watson had married in November, 1886[1], and bought a medical practice in Kensington, moving out of the famous apartment in Baker Street. Nevertheless he kept in close touch with Holmes and was on hand when, in May, 1887, a strange and anonymous masked man, claiming to be the 'Count von Kramm'[2] called. Sherlock Holmes was, however, quick to see through the disguise and rapidly identified his visitor as the King of Bohemia, a young man of thirty[3], who was shortly to be married.

According to Watson's account, which he called *A Scandal in Bohemia*, the forthcoming marriage was at the root of the problem. In the past the King had had an affair with a woman called Irene Adler, writing compromising letters and allowing a photograph[4] to be taken showing them together. The King claimed that Miss Adler was using the letter and picture to threaten him and he had been unable to persuade her to return them.

Holmes listened to all this with no apparent doubts. He got Watson to look up the entry for Adler, Irene[5], in his index, a

---

1) Watson's first wife, according to research by W. S. Baring-Gould, was Miss Constance Adams of San Francisco. Watson visited the city between 1884 and 1886, travelling to the United States in 1883 after learning that his brother was seriously ill. He met Miss Adams in 1884, became engaged to her in 1885 and returned to London with her in 1886. They were married at St George's, Hanover Square, London on 1st November. (*Sherlock Holmes, A Biography*, W.S.Baring-Gould, London 1963).
2) The King has been identified as Prince Albert Edward, Prince of Wales and later King Edward VII. (*A Scandal in Identity, Profile by Gaslight*, Edgar W. Smith, New York 1944).
3) Prince Albert was, in fact, 46 years old in 1887.
4) Eastman did not invent transparent photographic film until 1888 so this picture must have been taken using a glass plate.
5) Irene Adler may have been the sister of the American lecturer and adventurer Felix Adler who was born in Germany in 1851.

system for 'docketing all paragraphs concerning men and things', immediately after the King had described her as 'an adventuress'. Whether it was to see if the King's opinion was borne out, or simply to ascertain what information there was about her, we shall never know.

But all Sherlock Holmes learned from the index was that Miss Adler had been born in New Jersey in 1858, had had a distinguished career as an opera singer and had now retired from the stage. She had sung at La Scala[6] and most recently had been *prima donna* at the Imperial Opera of Warsaw. There was no mention of her being 'an adventuress', the Victorian term for a superior type of prostitute.

Miss Adler's reputation however did not daunt Holmes. Taking the King's story at face value he made his first suggestion on how to get the photograph back; the letters could be dismissed as forgeries. "Your Majesty must pay. It must be bought."

But that had already been tried. "She will not sell," explained the King.

In that case there was only one thing to do. "Stolen then," said Sherlock Holmes.

There is something highly questionable about suggesting theft as a solution to a client's problem. And what a client. A man who had appeared in a black comic-opera mask, adopted a false identity and made the totally unsupported claim that a world-famous opera singer was attempting to ruin his forthcoming marriage by threatening to reveal details of an earlier affair.

The King gave no motive for Irene Adler's supposed wish to see his planned marriage founder, save to suggest that she would go to any lengths to prevent him marrying another woman, but he did admit to taking fairly drastic measures to secure the return of his letters and the incriminating picture. "Twice burglars in my pay ransacked her house. Once we diverted her luggage when she travelled. Twice she has been waylaid."

Sherlock Holmes was unworried by the illegalities that had

6) *Teatro alla Scala*, Milan, Italy.

already taken place and about those which he knew he would have to commit. Neither was he concerned about substantiating the King's story, and nor did he seem to consider whether the cause was justifiable.

He had other things on his mind. "Then, as to money?"

Holmes's main concern was how much there was in it for him. Indeed, even before the King arrived, Holmes, upon seeing his client's brougham outside remarked: "There's money in this case, Watson, if nothing else."

The King airily said that Holmes had *carte blanche*. This, however, was not good enough. Sherlock Holmes may have trusted his client's story without any checking, but he did not trust him to pay his bill, or so it would seem. He persisted: "And for present expenses."

Eventually the King parted with three hundred pounds in gold and a further seven hundred in notes. A substantial sum in a period when a bachelor could live fairly comfortably on two hundred pounds a year[7].

Holmes then set off to earn his money. First a spying mission to the Adler house[8] in London. He was disguised and during the course of this he was drawn in as a witness to a wedding; the bride and groom were Irene Adler and Godfrey Norton, a barrister[9]. Should anything have made Holmes question the King's story it was this. Why should Miss Adler wish to stop the King marrying any other woman when she was being married herself?

This was a fact which rocked the whole of the King's story. Certainly we can accept that Miss Adler, a woman scorned would want her revenge on the man who wronged her. No doubt a wronged woman would feel totally justified in exacting vengeance by ruining the King's planned marriage. But a woman about to be married? Is it really credible that she would still want to see her erstwhile lover's marriage ruined? Hardly, unless the wrong he had done her was unusually savage.

7) Watson's army pension in 1880 was £210. 10s 0d [£210.50] per annum.
8) Briony Lodge, Serpentine Avenue, St John's Wood, London.
9) Norton lived and practised in the Inner Temple.

If things were as the King had claimed, and if Miss Adler were in fact an 'adventuress', she would hardly have been in a position to complain at her treatment. And indeed, the public scandal which the King alleged Miss Adler was planning would hardly contribute to her own happiness with the lawyer Norton.

This was certainly a state of affairs which a scrupulous private inquiry agent should have taken up with his client. Holmes, however, questioned nothing. He simply returned to Baker Street and, in a rather strange conversation, asked Watson to join him in the next stage of the case.

"You don't mind breaking the law?" said Holmes.

"Not in the least," replied Watson.

"Nor running a chance of arrest?"

Watson qualified his answer a little. "Not in a good cause," he said.

Whether recovering by illegal means a packet of compromising letters for a foreign King constituted a good cause, Watson didn't say. But Holmes, with more than a touch of irony, gave him his answer. "Oh, the cause is excellent."

That is not quite the way you would expect him to answer in the circumstances. By no stretch of the imagination can the cause be described as 'excellent'. Justified, perhaps, if you accept the King as a wronged man whose happiness is in peril. Possibly 'the only answer', if you feel there are inherent dangers to peace should the King's proposed marriage to the daughter of the King of Scandinavia fall through.

But to reply "Oh, the cause is excellent" could be nothing more than irony. Unless, of course, Sherlock Holmes was referring to his own cause.

He had, after all, already collected one thousand pounds and there was the prospect of much more to come. The King had declared: "I would give one of the provinces of my kingdom to have that photograph."

Holmes was interested, not in the rights and wrongs of the case, but in the money he could make out of it.

First, however, he had to get hold of the picture. To this end he and Watson went to Miss Adler's house in St. John's Wood where a number of people (Holmes had put some of the King's money as well as his own organisation to effective use) were in the street. A scuffle began and Holmes, disguised as a clergyman, was apparently injured and was carried inside the house.

Watson, obeying instructions, lobbed a smoke bomb through the window and the stage was set for Holmes to recover the photograph.

The plan was that Irene Adler, thinking the house was on fire, would rush to where the picture and the letters were hidden, Holmes would seize them from her and make off to return them to the King.

But oddly, although everything went as intended, when Holmes got back to Watson he did not have the papers with him, although he said he had found where they were hidden. His explanation was curiously weak in light of what was to follow.

Holmes claimed that everything went according to plan; he saw Irene Adler go to the hiding place when the fire alarm was given and take out the photograph. But then Holmes - for reasons best known to himself - told her the fire was a false alarm and she put the picture back in its hiding place and left the room.

"I hesitated whether to try to secure the photograph at once; but the coachman had come in and, as he was watching me narrowly, it seemed safer to wait," explained Holmes.

It is not an explanation that holds water. First there was no reason for Holmes to tell Irene Adler that it was a false alarm. He could, after all, have stuck to the original plan and simply snatched the picture from her. It certainly was not going to be safer to wait. He had already tricked his way into her house and, by leaving without the evidence, Holmes was faced with the problem of having to get inside once more.

And this time Irene Adler would be much more on her guard.

According to Watson, Holmes waited until the following day and then, along with the King, went to the house again and demanded to see Irene Adler. Of course they were too late. Alerted by the false fire alarm, she had gone, together with her new husband, leaving behind only a letter. In it she said that she had recognised Holmes, despite his disguise. She added that the King had 'cruelly wronged' her and that she was keeping the papers to 'safeguard' herself from 'future steps' by the King.

It can have been no surprise to Sherlock Holmes that she had gone. She would have realised that the fake fire had been yet another ruse by the King to get hold of the picture and the letters. She had, after all, been accosted by people in the pay of the King already, her luggage had been searched and her house burgled more than once. Even if she had decided to stay she would, at the very least, have changed the hiding place.

But it was Holmes's curious conduct in leaving the house when the picture was almost within his grasp and starting all over again the next day that we must question. It was hardly a logical act for so logical a man. What did he think he was waiting for? How did he hope to persuade Miss Adler to part with the picture?

Could he have restrained himself from just seizing the photograph when he first saw it? Surely not. He must have taken the picture at the time of the fire alarm. Doubtless he told Irene Adler to go while the going was good, as without the picture and the letters she had no protection against the King's anger. Holmes would have then had a little time in hand. No doubt the letters which were together with the photograph contained a sample of Miss Adler's handwriting and it would have been the work of a few minutes for Holmes to fabricate the letter, purporting to be from Irene Adler, which was eventually put in the hiding place.

Forged letters had, of course, been on Holmes's mind right at the beginning of the affair. When the King first visited Baker Street, Holmes had advised him that only the photograph was important. The letters, he said, could be dismissed as forgeries.

The letter found in the hiding place which talked of Miss Adler safeguarding herself from 'future steps' by the King does not ring quite true. The only use to which she could have put the letters and the photograph was to prevent the King's forthcoming wedding to the daughter of the King of Scandinavia. Once the marriage had taken place revelations about the King's past private life would have been embarrassing and relations might have been strained between Bohemia and Scandinavia, but little more.

The marriage would have been a *fait accompli* and the photograph would have lost its importance. Naturally after the wedding the two royal houses would have joined in trying to hush up any scandal. The King of Scandinavia may have felt that he should not be on speaking terms with his new son-in-law, but that state of affairs is not uncommon even in less exalted houses and eventually blows over.

The photograph would have been unlikely, then, to have safeguarded Miss Adler from future action by the King. In any case her possession of it had not prevented the King trying to get it back by all the means at his disposal. It was a vain hope to think it would protect her.

There was one other thing for Sherlock Holmes to do before telling Watson and the King of the arrangements for the next day. For his plan to be entirely convincing there had to be a member of Miss Adler's household to give a first-hand account to the King of what had happened.

Of course, Miss Adler had taken her servants away with her, so there was no such person. But Sherlock Holmes planned to provide one. At the same time as he had hired the group of people who caused the diversion in the street prior to the fake fire alarm, he had hired an elderly woman who was to play the part of housekeeper. She was almost certainly the mysterious 'Mrs. Turner' who figures in *A Scandal in Bohemia* as part of the Baker Street household. Since Mrs. Turner had a major speaking rôle in the drama that Sherlock Holmes was stage-managing, he would have taken her to Baker Street for some schooling in her role. Mrs. Hudson would have shown her how a housekeeper behaved and Holmes would have instructed her in her part. She appears only this once in Watson's reminiscences and it would

Irene Adler. To Sherlock Holmes she was always *the* woman.

appear that the doctor's only contact with her at Baker Street was the one occasion upon which she brought in a tray while he was there. It is therefore unlikely that she would have been recognised by him the following day. A simple disguise, a wig perhaps, would have rendered her a different person.

Mrs. Turner's rôle would have been to remain at Irene Adler's house and open the door to Holmes, Watson and the King. She had to tell Holmes that her mistress had gone, but had left word that Sherlock Holmes was expected. This simple device would fix quite clearly in the minds of the King and Dr. Watson - should there have been any doubt - that Holmes's account of the events of the previous day had been true.

Holmes could then 'discover' the letter he had forged and which said that he had been recognised (a clever and convincing touch). His story were therefore corroborated by both the housekeeper and the letter: yet both were fakes. Holmes now had the papers and the picture in his possession. Irene Adler had disappeared with her husband and, as far as we know, never crossed Sherlock Holmes's path again.

The King was quite happy at the way things turned out. Thinking that Irene Adler was just holding on to the evidence to protect herself, he regarded the picture as safe 'as if it were in the fire'. He offered Holmes an emerald ring as a reward, but the detective, who was expecting more after the King's expansive 'province of my kingdom' statement a little earlier, now chose to act petulantly. He hinted that he disapproved of the King's behaviour towards Miss Adler and pretended that he was totally affronted at being mixed up in the affair at all.

He had left it a little late to be upset. He knew from the King's original brief what he should expect and went into the matter quite happily. Nothing had happened that should have changed his attitude. But when the King asked Holmes what he wanted as a reward for sorting the case out, there was a snub from the detective. Just a memento, said Holmes, of Irene Adler. Then, ignoring the King's out-stretched hand, he gave a small bow and left for Baker Street.

That was not quite the end of the matter, however. Holmes changed his mind about the King's reward for, five months later, at the time of *A Case of Identity*, he showed Watson a snuff box of old gold with a 'great amethyst' in the centre of the lid. "A little souvenir from the King of Bohemia in return for my assistance in the case of the Irene Adler papers," he said.

It is unlikely after Holmes's snub that the King took it upon himself to persist with trying to reward the detective for his help. After all, he had not even got the papers back and had already handed over one thousand pounds. So when did Holmes collect the snuff box?

There can be little doubt that after the King had returned to the Langham Hotel[10] and Watson had returned to his wife, Sherlock Holmes had Mrs. Hudson whistle for a hansom cab.

The King would have been surprised to see Holmes so soon, but the reason for the visit would have rapidly become clear. The papers were now for sale. It would not cost the King a province of his kingdom, but the price would not be cheap.

To Holmes's surprise the King's relief at getting the papers back would have overcome his distaste for the method. He would have gladly paid Holmes's price in cash and willingly handed over the gold snuff box. 'I did tell you, Mr. Holmes, that you had but to name your own reward.'

This time as Holmes took his leave, the snuff box in his pocket and the King's money secreted about him, it was the King of Bohemia who failed to notice the outstretched hand. A King may shake the hand of the world's first and greatest consulting detective, a man at the pinnacle of his profession, but he would not soil his palm on the hand of a common tradesman.

A Scandal in Bohemia gave a clear indication of the way Sherlock Holmes was prepared to behave. He was willing to undertake criminal acts and break the law, not in the best interests of society, but in the interests of his own pocket. And his client was not always safe from him. The accepted image of Sherlock

---
10) For many years part of the BBC, the Langham re-opened as an hotel in 1990.

Holmes as an honourable and talented man doing his best to see that the interests of justice are served just will not do.

In *The Beryl Coronet* in 1890 Sherlock Holmes is again seen acting in the best interests of his own bank account. This concerned the theft of a valuable gem from the home of Mr. Alexander Holder, a banker, who had accepted it as security for a short term loan from a person whose name was 'a household word all over the earth - one of the highest, noblest, most exalted names in England'. The client was the banker. He suspected his son, Arthur, to be the thief and wanted Holmes to get the coronet back and avoid a scandal. All the circumstantial evidence pointed to the son but, nevertheless, tracks in the snow revealed the thief to be the banker's niece, an orphan who lived with the family as an adopted daughter. She had taken the jewel and handed it to her lover, Sir George Burnwell.

Holmes dealt with the affair quite efficiently, recovering the coronet, pointing out the guilty parties and, in the words of the banker, saving 'England from a great public scandal'. The scandal would have been if it had ever become public knowledge that the famous person who had left the coronet as security was in the habit of borrowing money. He had made it clear that it was a highly confidential matter.

But it was Holmes's conduct in recovering the jewel that does not bear close examination. He reported that he caught up with Sir George Burnwell, 'a man of evil reputation' and told him "we would give him a price for the stones he held - a thousand pounds apiece". Holmes made the offer in this way because the coronet had been damaged and the stones detached. However, since he claimed he was holding a pistol to Sir George's head during the conversation, it is curious that he should have felt the need to offer money at all. His explanation was that he was aware a prosecution must be avoided to avert a scandal and he knew that Sir George was astute enough to see 'our hands were tied'.

But were Holmes's hands tied to the extent he allowed the banker to think? A man with a gun at his head is unlikely to feel in a strong position and would be very likely simply to hand over the property. According to Holmes, however, he regretted missing the chance to do a deal: "Why dash it all, I've let them go at six hundred for the three."

Holmes claimed he managed to get the name of the receiver who had bought them from Burnwell and 'after much chaffering I got our stones at a thousand apiece'. Holder was delighted and had his cheque book at the ready. "Better make it out for four thousand pounds," advised Holmes.

The client was perhaps so overwhelmed that it did not occur to him that it was strange Holmes should have found it necessary to pay the receiver, even to avoid a scandal. A receiver is a known dealer in stolen property. He knew when he bought the gems that they were stolen. If they had not been he would never have been offered them, and certainly not at such a derisory price. What is more, since professional receivers are not in the habit of doing business with people they do not know, especially if the items are expensive, it is certain that Sir George Burnwell was known to the receiver. If the receiver wanted to go to the trouble of finding out where the stones had come from he probably would have been able to. He may even have got a shrewd idea who the important person was who had left them with the banker, but what good would it have done him? What was the word of a known dealer in stolen property, even if supported by the blackguard Sir George Burnwell, against the highest in the land and the most respected? Had Holmes simply taken the jewels back at gun-point, the aggrieved receiver might have felt upset, but he was hardly in a position to make trouble. If he said anything, or complained, he was simply admitting that he had bought stolen jewels. No-one would pay serious attention to his allegations. The same applied to Burnwell. He could not make any allegations without admitting he had stolen the gems.

Holmes could have achieved nothing by paying to get the stones back. They were stolen and the receiver knew they were stolen. He would, without doubt, have handed them back once

Holmes told him there would be no prosecution. At the very most Holmes might have given him six hundred pounds for them, compensating him for what he had paid Burnwell. But three thousand pounds was, to say the least, a little generous.

In fact, there can be little doubt that Holmes just repossessed the stones and told the receiver to count himself lucky the police were not being called. The three thousand pounds was a bonus for Sherlock Holmes. After all, he had all the elements of the scandal in the palm of his hand. His client was in no better position to argue about the three thousand pounds than about the one thousand which Holmes demanded as his fee. In any case four thousand pounds was a reasonable price to avoid ruin. The banker could afford it and had said as much when he consulted Holmes.

Sherlock Holmes's fees were large, of that there is no doubt, but then, the people he worked for were rich. They were able to pay whatever he asked, and if he sometimes helped himself to a client's cash, well, they could afford that too.

By the late 1880s Sherlock Holmes had become a man known and trusted by rich and influential people. When a cover-up was needed or a scandal loomed it was to 221B Baker Street they would go, and indeed some of the best known and most eminent people in Victorian England trod the seventeen steps up to the door of Holmes's sitting room. Their confidence in his discretion had made Sherlock Holmes a successful and wealthy man, yet a decade earlier he had been poverty-stricken and living on his wits.

CHAPTER TWO

A Study in Childhood

When Holmes met Watson in January, 1881, they were both searching for the same thing: somewhere comfortable, yet reasonably priced, to live. Neither could afford the whole of the rent of the Baker Street apartment on his own, but together they could manage. Watson had his army pension which amounted to 11s.6d. (57½p)[1] a day, or just over £4 a week, and Holmes it would appear was in a similar position.

But a little over a year earlier, Sherlock Holmes had been quite poor. In October 1879 he had told his former fellow student, Reginald Musgrave: "I am living on my wits."[2]

Yet the Holmes family was undoubtedly well-off. The little that is known of them makes this quite clear. "My ancestors were country squires, who appear to have led the same life as is natural to their class," Holmes told Watson in *The Greek Interpreter*. Country squires, of course, are not notably poor, but there is no guarantee that the wealth of the ancestor will descend to the immediate family. However, we know from *The Gloria Scott* and *The Musgrave Ritual* that Sherlock Holmes went to university. Mycroft Holmes, Sherlock's elder brother, also received a college education. There is no specific reference to Mycroft's education in any of Watson's accounts, but it is hardly likely that a father would send his younger son to university after failing to send his equally-gifted older boy. Also Mycroft was to assume a senior Whitehall appointment[3] that would not have gone to a non-graduate.

---

1) Watson tells us in *A Study in Scarlet* that he was 'as free as the air - or as free an an income of eleven shillings and sixpence a day will permit a man to be'.
2) *The Musgrave Ritual*.
3) Sherlock Holmes told Watson in *The Bruce-Partington Plans* that Mycroft was 'the

Sending two sons to university was not an inexpensive undertaking and the conclusion we must draw is that the family was in a position to spend a fair amount of money on tuition fees, books and maintaining the boys while they were at college.

So how did it happen that Sherlock Holmes, the son of a well-to-do family, who had spent a privileged period at university, found himself at the age of twenty-seven, unable to afford the rent of a decent apartment[4]?

By 1881 he had already built up a limited practice as a private detective, but he was not yet established and his income from this source would have been small and irregular, certainly not enough to pay rent of about £4 a week for the Baker Street rooms, even though meals were included.

In his meticulously researched biography of Sherlock Holmes, William Baring-Gould contended that during his time at university Holmes had a serious disagreement with his father which led to young Sherlock being cut off from the family - or as near to it as made no difference. He had no capital and was left with only a small allowance upon which to live. Baring-Gould thinks the cause of the disagreement was Sherlock's determination to become a detective. His father, according to Baring-Gould, found this unacceptable since he wanted the boy to be an engineer.

True, sons have been disinherited for less, but if we look more closely at the early years of Holmes's life, as revealed by Baring-Gould, another, more probable, explanation becomes apparent.

Sherlock Holmes was born on 6th January, 1854. For many years his early childhood remained a mystery, but Baring-Gould's

most indispensable man in the country'. He earned £450 a year, remained a subordinate and had no ambition of any kind. According to Sherlock, he had the 'tidiest and most orderly brain, with the greatest capacity for storing facts, of any man living'. He used his abilities by acting as a clearing house for Government information. "Again and again his word has decided the national policy," said Sherlock, who also claimed that 'occasionally he is the Government'.

4)   At this time Holmes was living in Montague Street, near the British Museum.

biography, published in 1962, filled in the previously unknown details. His parents were identified as Siger and Violet Holmes and the family lived at a farm known as "Mycroft" in the North Riding of Yorkshire.

Sherlock Holmes revealed to Watson in *The Greek Interpreter* the existence of his brother, Mycroft (presumably called after the farmstead), who was seven years his senior, but there is also evidence to suggest that there was a third brother, Sherrinford, who had been born a couple of years before Mycroft, in 1845. Significantly, however, there is a total absence of any reference to Sherrinford in any of Watson's reminiscences.

The most likely explanation is that Sherrinford died while still a child, probably before the birth of Sherlock. If we look at the dates of the births of the Holmes brothers, we can see that there was a gap of two years between Sherrinford and Mycroft. Yet it was a full seven years before the third son, Sherlock, was born. This is a slight inconsistency, nothing more. But this, and the lack of any mention of Sherrinford in Watson's chronicles, gives a clear indication of a certain course of events.

Shortly after Sherlock's birth, his father took the family on the first of a series of long journeys through Europe and if we take this, together with the absolute horror of any physical activity that Mycroft possessed later in life, a hypothesis begins to emerge.

Young Sherrinford probably died in 1852 at the age of seven. Possibly he fell from a pony, or perhaps he slipped on the bank of a river or on the bough of a tree. It was an accident that was to influence the whole of Mycroft Holmes' life, and it would have a devastating effect on the yet unborn Sherlock.

Siger Holmes took the death of his son especially hard and for months guilt that he had not prevented the accident, and remorse, played on his mind. When the new baby, Sherlock, was born a little less than two years after the tragedy, Siger had already changed from a warm, outgoing man to the harsh, introverted and withdrawn person he was to remain for the rest of his days.

For young Mycroft, the death of his brother would remain with him forever, associated permanently in his mind with physical activity and danger. From that moment he showed a reluctance to join in games or sport. He had no wish to ride, hunt, fish, shoot or even join his mother in their former much-loved pastime of taking long walks across the dales. But if Mycroft's life was scarred by the accident, his father's was mutilated.

Violet may well have thought that the new baby would, in some way, ease the burden that Siger was carrying. Perhaps even a well-meaning family physician had advised that this would be the case. If so, it was a mistake. Siger showed little interest in the child. He did not even suggest a name, but left it to his wife to pick the old English *Sherlock*, meaning 'fair-haired'. Siger continued his rejection of his new son for over a year until finally it became too much for Violet. She wrote to her father, the well-known explorer Sir Edward Sherrinford (the Holmes' first son had been named after Violet's family) complaining about her husband's continuing odd behaviour.

Sir Edward, a distinguished man of action, would have taken immediate steps to rectify the situation. He would have made the journey to the Holmes estate as soon as he received the letter. Perhaps more advice was taken from the family doctor. Mr. Baring-Gould has established that on 7th July, 1855, Siger Holmes and his entire family boarded the steamship *Lerdo* bound for Bordeaux. From that it would appear the advice Sir Edward offered was that Siger should pull himself together and get away from Yorkshire for a while.

Siger seized upon the suggestion. He had come to hate the land that had taken his son from him and the family travelled to Pau in south western France, where they remained until 1858. Subsequently they went to stay with relatives, the Vernet family at Montpelier, but had to return to England towards the end of 1858 because of the illness, and eventual death, of Sir Edward.

Sherlock was now four years old and Mycroft eleven. Siger,

21

a well-educated man, had undertaken the education of Mycroft while the family was in France. He had still hardly spoken to Sherlock. The family remained in Yorkshire for a while after the death of Sir Edward, but Siger was unable to come to terms with living there and, in 1860, the family again returned to the Continent. But now Siger was unable to escape the memory of his dead son. Sherrinford haunted him as he led his family through Germany, Holland, Italy and Switzerland before returning to England in 1864.

Mycroft was now seventeen years old. No doubt Violet pointed out to her husband that their aimless wanderings could not continue. If Mycroft was going to get into a university, his education needed attention. She could have added that ten year old Sherlock needed to get into school. So far his education had been limited to teaching from his mother and that which he had been able to pick up himself.

Not least, Violet would have realised that Sherlock needed the company of boys of his own age. His brother was too old to be a totally satisfactory companion and, in any case, she would have felt that Sherlock needed to get away from the oppressive atmosphere which now dogged the family all the time. Siger's rejection of his son had never wavered and young Sherlock had met it first with uncomprehending distress, then with attempts to endear himself to his father and finally with hostility. Sherlock Holmes, although the family would never admit it, hated his father.

But Siger loved Mycroft and Violet's plea that the boy needed to prepare for university entrance made sense. Siger Holmes agreed to return to England, but he refused to go to Yorkshire and the family took a house in London.

Mycroft was enrolled in an establishment which would prepare him for Oxford, the university which Sherlock would also attend. The controversy over which university Sherlock Holmes attended has raged for many years. However, research by

Nicholas Utechin[5] has convincingly put him at St John's College, Oxford, though I would doubt that he entered at the age of fifteen, as Mr Utechin suggests.

Meanwhile, Sherlock went to a board school[6]. In many ways it was too late for him. The company of other children was unbearable after years of solitude and the ten year old boy began spending more time alone, often wandering the streets of south London. Baring-Gould has successfully established that about this time Sherlock became friendly with a man whose name is recorded only as 'Old Sherman', who kept a taxidermist shop in Lambeth. Here Sherlock would spend hours watching Sherman at his bizarre trade. The boy was fascinated with the idea of preserving and stuffing animals and birds and it was not long before he began to take an interest in the chemicals that were used in the process. The preservative used at that time included arsenic. Young Sherlock had first been interested in the art of the taxidermist, but his interest moved to the chemicals which were used and the properties which they possessed. He was interested in the antidotes to the poisons and those poisons which had no antidote. Soon he was spending hours at the old shop, occasionally carrying out small experiments of his own. Old Sherman would have watched with indulgent interest, surprised by finding a lad who was not revolted by the details of taxidermy and half hoping he had found an apprentice.

The time spent in the taxidermist shop set the groundwork for the spread of knowledge that Holmes was later to acquire.

The origins of his specialised knowledge, which Watson was to set out some years later, are in clear evidence: "Knowledge of botany - variable. Well up in belladonna, opium and poisons generally. Knowledge of chemistry - profound. Knowledge of anatomy - accurate, but unsystematic."[7]

5) *Sherlock Holmes at Oxford*, Nicholas Utechin, Oxford 1977.
6) A public elementary school, so called because it was managed by a locally elected school board.
7) *A Study in Scarlet*

It was about this time that Sherlock Holmes became seriously ill. He collapsed in the winter of 1866 and medical advice prompted the family to leave London and set up home in Yorkshire once more. Mycroft was by this time safely off to Oxford and there was no reason to keep Siger in London. He was unwilling to return to the scene of the tragedy that had occurred all those years earlier, but at Violet's urging, the family went.

The illness which affected Sherlock has been explained by others in the terms of the collapses which happened later in his life and on more than one occasion ended in an enforced rest. The truth of the matter was somewhat different.

Watson's friend Stamford before making the famous introduction had Sherlock Holmes fairly well summed up. "Holmes is a little too scientific for my tastes - it approaches to cold bloodedness. I could imagine his giving a friend a little pinch of the latest vegetable alkaloid, not out of malevolence, you understand, but simply out of a spirit of inquiry in order to have an accurate idea of the effects. To do him justice, I think he would take it himself with just the same readiness."[8]

The young Sherlock, whose inquiring nature had led him to probe the properties and effects of poisons had been doing just that. Violet would have guessed what he had been doing, hence her eagerness to move out of London and away from Old Sherman's shop. Back in Yorkshire Sherlock Holmes was enrolled in the local grammar school and Violet no doubt thought the poison episode was at an end.

But arsenic was readily available in farmyards where it was widely used as a rat poison, so Sherlock had no trouble getting supplies. He also spent time in the countryside searching for, and experimenting with, certain plants, among them belladonna.

Two years later Sherlock received a beating from his schoolmaster for failing a test in literature. It was the latest in a

8)   *Ibid*

long line of beatings from the same man and it was to be the last. A few days later the schoolmaster lay between life and death, his body consumed by an unknown illness. It was only when the man's life appeared to be slipping away that Sherlock spoke. He told his mother the nature of the poison and the antidote.

The schoolmaster survived and Sherlock was soundly thrashed by his father. However, it was not the end of the affair. Local people began to connect the Holmes family's correct diagnosis of the schoolmaster's illness with young Sherlock's interest in poisons. There had also been the unexplained deaths of numerous small animals in the area.

Gossip began to circulate. After all, it had been Sherlock Holmes's schoolmaster who was the victim. Siger decided the best thing was to leave the district while things settled down, and the family set off once more for the south of France. A tutor was engaged and the family did not return to England until 1872 when Sherlock entered St. John's College, Oxford.

Holmes has admitted he made only one friend in his time at university, but that may well be something of an exaggeration. True, his childhood, by its wandering nature, and the rejection by his father had made Sherlock Holmes a man who found it difficult to form relationships, but it has been claimed by Baring-Gould that he may have formed a friendship while at Oxford with Charles Lutwidge Dodgson, otherwise Lewis Carroll, who in 1865 had published *Alice's Adventures in Wonderland*. Dodgson, a devoted theatre and opera lover, may have introduced Holmes to any number of the actors and actresses who visited the university town, or it may simply have been a natural inclination that took Holmes into what would have been considered the lower social orders.

Holmes's interest in chemicals, particularly the opiates, would have made him a popular fellow with certain of his colleagues at university. Thomas de Quincy, whose *Confessions of an English Opium Eater* had been first published in serial form in 1821 and who had been an Oxford man, had died at the age of 74 in 1859, but his famous book still awakened in students the desire to experiment with narcotics. There would have been frequent small gatherings in the rooms of Holmes or other undergraduates and, for the first time, Sherlock Holmes would have had willing subjects, other than himself, to administer the substances to. It would have been about this time that he noticed certain narcotics created dependencies which were sometimes difficult to shake off.

The drug-taking sessions introduced Holmes to a circle of acquaintances who demanded little. The women of the group were actresses or even the ladies of the town who paraded the High. There was no demand for a lasting relationship and Sherlock Holmes, still the victim of his lonely childhood, was content.

It was about two years after Holmes went to Oxford that scandal flared. A young woman became seriously ill in his rooms after she had taken a drug. A doctor was called and there was a college inquiry. Things were black for Holmes: the drug-taking sessions, the women and an erratic work record pointed in just one direction. He packed his things and, still an undergraduate, took the train to London. A telegram to Mycroft, who was now a junior Government employee, ensured that Holmes had somewhere to go when he arrived in the metropolis. Mycroft had found an apartment for Sherlock in Montague Street, Bloomsbury.

Holmes arrived to find his father waiting for him. It had been Siger's intention to attempt a reconciliation with his son. Mycroft had told Violet what had happened and she in turn had told Siger, but she had told him in such a way that he saw his treatment of Sherlock as a child had led to the present situation. Unwillingly at first, but then with some sense of hopeful anticipation, Siger had made the journey to London to wait for Sherlock in Montague Street.

Siger was furious when Sherlock arrived accompanied by the woman, some years his senior, who had been at the centre of the Oxford scandal. "I came to try and help you," he shouted. "But you will get rid of that whore before I will speak with you."

Unfortunately after two years of independence at Oxford,

Sherlock decided it was time to stand up to his father.

"I am afraid I am unable to do that, father," he said, languidly gazing at Siger for what was to be the last time. "You see I married her this morning." Stunned, his father turned on his heel and left the room. The following day a letter told Sherlock that while Siger would continue his errant son's small allowance, he never wanted to see him again.

Whether or not Sherlock's claim that he had married the woman was the truth or mere bravado is a matter for conjecture. The eminent author Michael Harrison claimed to have discovered a listing in the *London Post Office Directory* for 1878 showing that the tenant of No.24 Montague Street was a 'Mrs. Holmes'[9]. It may well be that this is the woman Sherlock brought with him from Oxford, but whether they ever went through a marriage ceremony is another matter, Most important is that the woman had led to a final split between Sherlock and his father.

It was 1875. Sherlock Holmes had an apartment in London, no degree, a small income and was living with a woman who, until a few days earlier, had been little better than a prostitute in Oxford. It was not a promising situation for a young man just turned 21.

It was then that he remembered Victor Trevor. A year earlier, Trevor, a fellow undergraduate at Oxford, had invited Holmes to stay with him at his home in Norfolk. During the course of that visit Holmes was able to act in the attempted blackmail of Trevor's elderly father and after a demonstration of his powers of observation and deduction, the senior Trevor had told him that he should become a detective[10]. Now, living in the capital with few prospects and little money Holmes thought back to that piece of advice. Here was a chance to hire out his services and get a fairly quick return. It was just what he needed.

It was not to be as easy as Holmes perhaps first imagined. He was skilled in the art of observation and deduction, but what he

9) *The World of Sherlock Holmes*, Michael Harrison, London 1973.
10) *The Gloria Scott*

needed were clients and they were slow to come. The woman was eventually to leave him; living with a pauper in London was not her idea of the good life. But Holmes decided that to become a private inquiry agent was now the best road for him to take. It was a road that eventually took him to the laboratory at St. Bartholomew's Hospital and his meeting with Dr. John H. Watson. Almost immediately they decided to move into the suite of rooms in Baker Street which Holmes had found.

Little did either man realise the legend they were about to create.

A photograph said to be of the Holmes brothers, Mycroft and Sherlock.

CHAPTER THREE

A Case of Ambition

Victor Trevor's father had told the young Sherlock Holmes: "It seems to me that all the detectives of fact and fancy, sir, would be children in your hands. That's your line of life, sir ..."

Much later Holmes was to tell Watson that Trevor's words, in September, 1874, had been "the very first thing which ever made me feel that a profession might be made out of what had up to that time been the merest hobby".

He was to act on Trevor's advice when faced with the need to make a living in London in 1875. We can only guess at the type of problem which would have been brought to Holmes in the years immediately after he made his decision to become an inquiry agent, but we can be sure that he was not dealing with the upper echelons of society. And we may also be fairly sure that he counted his fees in shillings rather than in guineas. No doubt he would have scratched a living by taking, like many other inquiry agents at the time, assignments as a guard for property or persons, seeking missing wives or husbands, lost purses or wallets. Sherlock Holmes would have discovered, again like many other inquiry agents, that the one thing a private detective has most difficulty in finding is a client. His leisure time at Montague Street was, as he told Watson, 'too abundant'[1].

Reginald Musgrave, who called on Holmes on 2nd October, 1879, had known Sherlock Holmes slightly at Oxford and had been impressed by the deductive powers that he had been only too happy to demonstrate. "I understand, Holmes, you are turning to

1)   *The Musgrave Ritual*

practical ends those powers with which you used to amaze us."

He did not, however, ask Holmes whether he was making a success of it. It probably was not necessary. Montague Street in the 1870s was not one of London's most fashionable districts. It was an area of small hotels and boarding houses and not the kind of place you would expect to find someone who was doing well. Sherlock Holmes was now approaching twenty-four years of age, college was a long way behind him, and it was time he was showing some evidence of material progress.

His apartment may well have revealed his poverty even more than the district in which it was situated. Although Holmes told Watson: "When I first came up to London I had rooms in Montague Street", we should note that Reginald Musgrave walked into Holmes's '*room* in Montague Street'.

Sherlock Holmes was clearly not doing very well. Musgrave, on the other hand, was doing very well indeed. He had inherited the family estates, which he was managing, and had become Member of Parliament for his district. "My life has been a busy one," he told Holmes.

Sherlock Holmes, who could hardly find enough to occupy him at that time, could only reply: "I have taken to living on my wits."

The hint of apology in the response may well indicate that Holmes, whose previous contact with Musgrave had been in the egalitarian surroundings of college, was feeling acute embarrassment that the 'scion of one of the oldest families in England' had turned up unexpectedly to find Holmes living in a single room in an unfashionable part of London. Under those circumstances Holmes was unable to pretend things were going as well as he would have liked. If he had been given some notice of Musgrave's intention to consult him, it is likely he would have suggested either that he would call on Musgrave or that they should meet somewhere convenient to both of them.

Reginald Musgrave may have been showing signs of regretting he had come. He would have noticed Holmes's embarrassment and could well have questioned whether he was making the right decision. Luckily for Holmes, Musgrave's doubts, were there any, were overcome and the affair of *The Musgrave Ritual* was eventually added to the Holmes legend.

Sherlock Holmes considered the case to be unique 'in the criminal records of this, or, I believe, any other country'. And he rightly pointed out that a collection of his 'trifling achievements' would be incomplete without a record of it.

The Musgrave Ritual concerned the mysterious goings-on at Hurlstone, Reginald Musgrave's ancestral home. The ritual of the title eventually gave the clue to the discovery of the ancient crown of the Kings of England, missing since the reign of Charles I. Musgrave's butler had seen the significance of the words of the ritual, giving the clue to the hiding place of the crown, and had been killed by his girl accomplice - for reasons of passion, not greed - after discovering the crown. His body subsequently fell back into the hiding place to be found later by Sherlock Holmes.

Whether this can be described as unique seems highly debatable. The discovery of the crown was certainly of archælogical interest and the murder of the butler would have interested the police, but a crime of passion was hardly unique. Holmes's investigation was workmanlike and his insight into the words of the ritual was shrewd, but the butler had already reached the same conclusion. The case itself was interesting in real terms for the discovery of the crown. It was not a significant criminal matter.

Why then should Sherlock Holmes, years later, be at pains to emphasise how important the case was?

Holmes himself supplied the answer. He pointed out that Musgrave was an aristocrat, of ancient family ('though his branch is a cadet one'). He was a man of wealth, keeping a considerable staff, he had estates and had become a Member of Parliament. In short, Musgrave was rich, powerful and acceptable in the greatest houses of England. Most important, he had a problem and was ready to place himself in the hands of Sherlock Holmes.

Wealth, power and vulnerability. These are the elements found time and again in Holmes's cases. Even late in his career in *The Priory School*, Holmes was unwilling to make time for the unprepossessing schoolmaster Dr. Thorneycroft Huxtable, yet when he heard that the client would really be the Duke of Holdernesse, one of the greatest and richest men in England, then his attitude changed entirely.

It was in the Musgrave case that he discovered and analyzed the elements necessary to enable him to become known as the greatest detective of all time.

He saw that to have rich and influential people consult him when they were at their most vulnerable could bring vast advantages. Even at the simplest level, he was more likely to get a big fee from a wealthy man. A poor man just was not able to pay. He was to tell Watson later that the Musgrave family kept the ancient crown at Hurlstone after its discovery 'though they had some legal bother and a considerable sum to pay before they were allowed to retain it'. The young Holmes saw that a large fortune and a famous name made all things possible. If the Musgraves wanted to keep the ancient crown of England they could. All it took was some 'legal bother' and a lot of money.

Apart from this valuable insight, Sherlock Holmes would also have received a substantial fee from Reginald Musgrave. The young aristocrat's delight at having the mystery cleared up, his pleasure at discovering the ancient crown, would have disposed him to making a handsome payment to Sherlock Holmes. He would, however, have been even more generous when he recalled the circumstances under which his old fellow student was living.

The rate at the time for returning lost or stolen articles was five or ten percent of their value. The ancient crown, of course, was beyond price, but Holmes's fee, it is safe to say, would have been in hundreds of guineas rather than shillings.

Now that Holmes had seen the profit in being retained by the rich, he determined that when the wealthy, famous and powerful were in trouble they would come to his door.

But how to go about it? Despite his large fee from Musgrave, Holmes was still not a wealthy man. He still lived in Bloomsbury and he still had no day to day contact with people like Reginald Musgrave.

Nevertheless Musgrave's generosity had given Holmes a little time. For a while at least, he would no longer be forced to live 'on his wits'. Now he had the money to concentrate on charting the path his career was taking and build up the more lucrative and respectable side of his practice. For the first time he was free of the pressure of not knowing where his next meal was coming from. He could give up the demeaning tasks that he, like all other inquiry agents of the time, were forced to accept: acting as security guard or strong arm man, pub bouncer or messenger.

It must have been tempting for him to use the fee from Musgrave to rent an office in Gray's Inn Road, Fleet Street or the Strand and attempt to encourage the lawyers from the nearby Inns of Court to make use of his services. That might have been a short cut to respectability, but Sherlock Holmes was wise enough to realise it would have been a gamble. With Musgrave's cash as capital and his small allowance he could do better.

His more profitable and most satisfying cases had come from old college friends, but clearly these would not be sufficient to make the basis of a successful practice. There had, as Holmes was the first to admit, been only three, and while there might be referrals it would be a long uphill struggle if he was to rely on this source of income. He needed to encourage more clients from the middle and upper classes.

His problem was that he had far too limited a circle of acquaintances. Were there a problem in the upper echelon of society, Sherlock Holmes was unlikely to know about it. The circles he moved in meant it was unlikely that he would hear gossip or get an early tip-off. And in any event, even if Holmes had received early information about a problem in high society, he was in no position to do anything about it.

His background, his inability even with a couple of years at

Oxford to supply adequate introductions and his humble Bloomsbury address were not in his favour. Even now his childhood was against him. In normal circumstances the son, even of a country squire like Siger, would have made childhood friends and contacts that would have lasted into adult life. But the wandering of the Holmes family meant that Sherlock had hardly met anyone in England, let alone made friends. And then he had missed out on school. A few years at public school would again have helped in making contacts, but Sherlock Holmes had never been to a public school, although his father could well have afforded to send him. The shadow of Sherrinford still hung over Sherlock Holmes's life.

But Holmes quickly identified his problem: he needed to widen his circle of acquaintances; he needed to become socially acceptable; he needed to make sure he had up-to-date information about the kind of case he would be interested in and, eventually, he would need a better address.

To become socially acceptable is not something that is easily accomplished at any time, In Victorian England it was near impossible. Everyone had his place and stayed there. But Holmes already had the answer. The Musgrave case had come from a fellow student. Holmes had known him at college. Consequently Musgrave, upon hearing that Holmes was willing to hire out his talent, had had few reservations about retaining him.

University had been the key. It was at Oxford that Sherlock Holmes had made his important contacts. Consequently with a small degree of financial security at his command, he resolved to return to college.

Clearly he could not return to Oxford. Holmes was operating in London and to leave the capital would have taken him away from the very people he wished to cultivate. Anyway, London had a perfectly satisfactory university and medical school.

Holmes knew that circulating among the students in London would give him an acceptability that was denied a down-at-heel private inquiry agent - a class notoriously short of status. It would give him contacts among the type of people he needed to know. Perhaps because he thought he would meet a better class of student there, or possibly simply because the facilities were more suitable to the course of study he intended to pursue, Sherlock Holmes enrolled himself in St. Bartholomew's Hospital medical school, not to train as a doctor but to study organic chemistry[2].

This done, Sherlock Holmes was well on the way. If he picked his university friends carefully he would have a wide circle of socially acceptable acquaintances, who could give him an introduction to important or influential people. He still, however, needed further information on criminal matters, the kind of information that was the preserve of the police and the underworld. Holmes already had some underworld contacts. You could not be a private inquiry agent in London then without them, since rewards were often offered for stolen goods. These obviously needed expanding. He also needed contacts in the police force.

Holmes set out to achieve all this. The one thing he did not do immediately was change his address. That would have stretched his still slender means too far and, in any case, as a financially hard pressed student he could still be accepted wherever he went. The bulk of his capital he could retain for future use. He must have decided this soon after the Musgrave case in October, 1879.

A study of organic chemistry is not a full degree course, and it is safe to assume that Sherlock Holmes would have been able to achieve much in a year. In fact he had achieved a great deal by the time he met Watson. That January day when the two were introduced was, coincidentally, the same day that Holmes discovered an infallible test for bloodstains.

By the time of the meeting with Watson, Sherlock Holmes's plan was well advanced. He was comfortably carrying out his research, and was looking for a better address. In *A Study in*

[2]   Holmes was at work in the laboratory at St Bartholomew's Hospital in London when he first met Watson. Bart's is one of the medical schools of the University of London.

Scarlet in March, 1881, we see that Holmes had established close contact with the police force and was familiar with the Scotland Yard detectives Lestrade and Gregson. He even received a letter from Gregson asking for an opinion on a murder and had a well-organised underworld intelligence service in the form of the street arab gang, the Baker Street Irregulars. He was also achieving a limited reputation, according to one London evening paper, the *Echo* of 7th March that year, 'as an amateur (who) has shown some talent in the detective line'.

There was one other thing which he had done. He had seen the way the private detective or inquiry agent was received, and had changed his profession. He would not, after all, join the grubby band of paid spies who jostled in the gutters of the city. He would be something quite different. Something unique. He would be a *consulting* detective.

Holmes told Watson early on in their friendship that when official or private detectives ran into difficulty they would consult Holmes, lay all the evidence before him and, because of his knowledge of the history of crime, he was generally able to help.

Of course, he said, there were occasions when he had to go out and get first hand evidence, but generally he would listen to a story, the client would listen to Holmes's comments and Holmes would then pocket his fee.

It was all nonsense, of course. He was an ordinary private detective and in the vast majority of the recorded cases Holmes operated in exactly the same way as any other private investigator.

The title 'consulting detective' was mere window dressing, An added encouragement for people like Mr. John Scott-Eccles in *Wisteria Lodge*, who was moved to remark: "Private detectives are a class with whom I have absolutely no sympathy ..."

When Sherlock Holmes, consulting detective, moved to Baker Street in 1881 his years of preparation wēre over. He had reached a turning point in his life.

CHAPTER FOUR

The Irregular Band

During the early years in Baker Street, Sherlock Holmes still had insufficient clients for a satisfactory practice, although things were improving. In 1881 he had the basis of the organisation that was to put him in such a strong position in the years ahead. His circle of acquaintances was widening comfortably and he had his underworld informants and police contacts. He also had his prestige Baker Street address which he shared with Dr. Watson, a man whose reputation was above reproach.

Nevertheless, this was still only the beginning. Holmes's business was growing, but it had yet to reach the level that he wanted. When he had decided to move to Baker Street he had not been in a position to afford the rent on his own and for some time to come he, like Watson, still had to watch his expenditure.

Watson's first account of Sherlock Holmes, *A Study in Scarlet*, takes place in 1881. The next report of one of Holmes's cases was *The Speckled Band* which took place in April, 1883, more than two years later. Yet Watson was to remark subsequently that, looking over his notes, it was no easy matter to select the best cases to report, since between 1882 and 1890 there were so many that were interesting.

Despite this, he reported no cases as having occurred in 1882 and only *The Speckled Band* in 1883. There followed a gap until October, 1886, when Holmes was involved in the affair of *The Resident Patient*. Two other cases in the same year were reported by Watson[1] and in 1887 there were details of eight adventures[2].

1) *The Noble Bachelor*; *The Second Stain*.
2) *The Reigate Squires*; *A Scandal in Bohemia*; *The Man with the Twisted Lip*; *The Five Orange Pips*; *A Case of Identity*; *The Red Headed League*; *The Dying Detective*; *The Blue Carbuncle*.

In 1888 Watson recorded five cases[3] and in the following year seven[4].

There is little doubt that things were fairly slow for Sherlock Holmes in the years immediately following his move to Baker Street. He does not appear to have had a continuous flow of work until 1886, but thereafter he seems to have been kept fairly busy.

Watson, although not giving details, also mentions some of the other cases of the period. Their frequency follows the same pattern as the recorded cases, confirming the pattern of a slow start, building up to a constant flow. There is mention by Watson of eight cases which took place in 1886[5] apart from those he reported in detail. In 1887 there were certainly fifteen additional cases[6] and in 1888, thirteen[7]. There were fewer in 1889[8], but the pattern is there. Holmes was not doing a lot between 1881 and 1886, but after that he worked continuously.

3) *The Valley of Fear*; *The Yellow Face*; *The Greek Interpreter*; *The Sign of Four*; *The Hound of the Baskervilles*.
4) *The Copper Beeches*; *The Boscombe Valley Mystery*; *The Stockbroker's Clerk*; *The Naval Treaty*; *The Cardboard Box*; *The Engineer's Thumb*; *The Crooked Man*.
5) The Delicate Case of the King of Scandinavia; The Service for Lord Backwater; The Case of the Woman at Margate; The Darlington Substitution Scandal; The Arnsworth Castle Business; The Little Problem of the Grosvenor Square Furniture Van; The Case of the Fishmonger; The Case of the Tide-Waiter.
6) The Summons to Odessa in the Case of the Trepoff Murder; The Delicate Affair of the Reigning Family of Holland; The Singular Adventure of the Atkinson Brothers at Tricomalee; The Netherland-Sumatra Company and the Colossal Schemes of Baron Maupertuis; The Adventure of the Paradol Chamber; The Adventure of the Amateur Mendicant; The Loss of the British Barque *Sophy Anderson*; The Singular Adventure of the Grice Patersons in the Island of Uffa; The Camberwell Poisoning Case; The Death of Mrs Stewart, of Lauder; The Case of Bert Stevens, the Terrible Murderer; The Saving of Colonel Prendergast in the Tankerville Club Scandal; The Three Occasions on which Holmes was Beaten by Men; The Missing Mr Etherege; The One or Two Little Skirmishes and Scores to Settle with Mr John Clay; The Dundas Separation Case; The Rather Intricate Matter from Marseilles; The Fate of Victor Savage.
7) The Two Cases in which Holmes helped Inspector MacDonald; The Little Affair of the Vatican Cameos; The Little Domestic Complication of Mrs Cecil Forrester; The Case of the Most Winning Woman Holmes Ever Knew; The Bishopsgate Jewel Case; The Little Case of Messenger-Manager Wilson; The Manor House Case; The French Will Case; The Blackmailing Case; The Atrocious Conduct of Colonel Upwood; The Abbas Parva Tragedy.
8) The Adventure of the Tired Captain; The Very Commonplace Little Murder; The Bogus Laundry Affair; The Locking-Up of Colonel Carruthers; Colonel Warburton's Madness; The Capture of Archie Stamford, the Forger.

This lack of activity in the early years is clearly shown in *The Speckled Band*. Holmes's client, Miss Helen Stoner, called at Baker Street at a quarter past seven in the morning. Watson was still asleep, yet Holmes had no compunction about waking him up. "What is it, then," asked Watson, "A fire?"

"No," replied Holmes triumphantly, "a client." This cannot be dismissed as simple surprise at the early arrival of Miss Stoner. If this had been the case, Holmes could have listened to her story before calling in Watson. After all, there was no guarantee she was not a lunatic. Clearly the arrival of a client at 221B Baker Street was not a daily event; Holmes was so excited by the appearance of Miss Stoner that he was unable to restrain himself from announcing it to the doctor.

Watson was next to take up the story of Sherlock Holmes with the case of *The Resident Patient*, which occurred in October, 1886. Things had changed dramatically in the intervening years, indicating that Holmes's strategy was becoming successful and he was by this time well established.

His client in this affair was Dr. Percy Trevelyan, who arrived in his own brougham and announced that his practice was in prestigious Brook Street. Trevelyan was just the sort of client that Holmes wanted. Wealthy and respected, a man who had had 'so distinguished a career'. But how had he come to Holmes's door?

"I am a London University man, you know." There was the connection. Holmes had haunted the university to widen his circle and Trevelyan's appearance was a direct result. He was a distinguished doctor and obviously had a distinguished list of patients. If Holmes made a success of Trevelyan's case then when the doctor heard of problems involving his patients that called for the services of a private detective rather than a physician, it was plain to whom he would send them. And a doctor is frequently the first person to hear of his patients' problems.

The Trevelyan case was the first indication that Holmes had broken into the kind of society that would give him the type of career he was seeking. But although it is the first recorded case of the type, there had been others[9]. Holmes was already acceptable to high society.

The affair of *The Resident Patient* reached a conclusion on 7th October, 1886, and on the following day *The Noble Bachelor* Lord Robert St. Simon, the second son of the Duke of Balmoral, was outlining to Sherlock Holmes the sorry tale of how he had lost his bride.

"Lord Backwater tells me that I may place implicit reliance upon your judgement and discretion," he had written to Holmes, adding, "Mr. Lestrade of Scotland Yard is acting in the matter already, but he assures me he sees no objection to your co-operation and that he even thinks it may be of some assistance."

Whether the idea that Lord Robert should consult Holmes came from Lestrade or Lord Backwater we can only guess. But clearly Lord Backwater knew Holmes and was willing to vouch for him. Holmes was now acceptable to the establishment and he told Lord Robert St. Simon that he had recently acted for the King of Scandinavia.

It is interesting to note that when Lord Robert St. Simon's letter asking for assistance arrived at Baker Street, Holmes had mistaken it for 'one of those unwelcome social summonses which call upon a man either to be bored or to lie'[10]. There can be no clearer indication of how things had changed.

And, in fact, four days later, on Tuesday, 12th October, Sherlock Holmes was involved in the 'most important international case which he has ever been called upon to handle'. Watson was reticent to discuss it at first and the account of *The Second Stain* was not published until the December of 1904, some eighteen years after the events, The clients were Lord Bellinger, twice Prime Minister of England, and his Secretary for European Affairs, the Right Honourable Trelawney Hope.

Here was Sherlock Holmes entertaining in his Baker Street rooms the two most powerful men in the country. The problem

---

9) The Delicate Case of the King of Scandinavia; The Service for Lord Backwater
10, *The Noble Bachelor.*

concerned a lost letter containing information that could have caused chaos in Europe. Holmes was able to recover it, learning incidentally that it had been taken by the European Secretary's wife, who was being blackmailed over an indiscretion. The letter was returned and Holmes agreed to keep quiet about the lady's part in the affair.

In a period of less than six years, Sherlock Holmes had climbed from an impoverished failure who had to watch every shilling to a man who was not only accepted, but trusted by the highest echelons of society, the aristocracy, the wealthy, the distinguished and the powerful.

He had achieved this by careful planning and prudent choice of friends and contacts. He had built an organisation to help him, an organisation that was to make Sherlock Holmes more powerful, more famous and probably as wealthy as any of them.

Much later, during the affair of *The Disappearance of Lady Frances Carfax*, Watson was to refer to Holmes's 'small, but very efficient organisation'. He meant, of course, the network of underworld informers and the corps of street arabs, the Baker Street Irregulars. However, we should not forget that Watson himself was an integral part of Holmes's organisation and that there were also a number of police officers willing to tip Holmes off for either financial reward or in exchange for a favour.

One of the more interesting of Holmes's informers was Langdale Pike, who acted as a 'human book of reference upon all matters of social scandal'. Watson, who clearly found him an unpleasant character, said; "This strange languid creature spent his waking hours in the bow window of a St. James's club, and was the receiving station, as well as the transmitter, for all the gossip of the metropolis."[11]

Pike made a living, according to Watson, by selling paragraphs to the gutter press. 'Holmes discreetly helped Langdale to knowledge, and on occasion was helped in turn.' He

11) *The Three Garridebs*.

was apparently an indispensable tool in Sherlock Holmes's trade.

Lower in the scale came those like Fred Porlock and Shinwell Johnson. In January, 1888, Holmes believed Porlock to be acting as 'the pilot fish with the shark, the jackal with the lion' and keeping Holmes in touch with the activities of his adversary Professor Moriarty[12]. Porlock received 'an occasional ten pound note' for his trouble.

Johnson was an ex-convict engaged by Holmes to supply information about the underworld. Watson remarks that 'with the glamour of his four convictions upon him, he had the entrée of every nightclub, doss house and gambling den in the town'.[13]

Naturally information about the network of informants who kept Holmes supplied with underworld news is hard to come by. All investigators must keep the names of their informants a close secret simply to protect them and Holmes was no exception. Doubtless Watson had no idea of the identity of the vast majority of Holmes's contacts.

He did eventually learn, however, that Holmes had a brother. Seven years Sherlock's senior, Mycroft Holmes occupied an important Government position. Holmes was unwilling even to talk about this informant. In September, 1888, almost nine years after he and Watson had decided to share the rooms in Baker Street, he still felt unable to be totally frank about his brother.

And it was not until 1895, when Holmes was asked to look into the matter of *The Bruce Partington Plans* that he was totally open about Mycroft.

Occasionally, said Holmes, his elder brother 'is the British Government'. He explained that he didn't tell Watson this before because "I did not know you so well in those days". He added that he had 'to be discreet'.

Finally it was clear. Holmes had a very high-level contact in the Government, a factor which may go a long way to explaining why, fairly early in his career, he was asked to undertake the

12) *The Valley of Fear.*
13) *The Illustrious Client.*

sensitive affair of the missing letter which Watson eventually wrote up as *The Second Stain*.

Some of Holmes's contacts will remain always shrouded in mystery. What, for example, was the connection, if any, between Hudson the seaman who 'disappeared completely and utterly' at the time of the *Gloria Scott* affair in 1874, and Mrs. Hudson, Holmes's long-suffering landlady? Husband and wife, brother and sister-in-law, or simply a coincidence of names? Was either of them, for example, connected with Morse Hudson who, in 1900, kept a shop in Kennington Road and was involved in the affair of *The Six Napoleons*?

Could Morse Hudson and Hudson the seaman be one and the same? Morse Hudson was described by Watson as 'a small, stout man with a red face and a peppery manner'.

The seaman was described by Sherlock Holmes. "A little weazened fellow, with a cringing manner and a shambling style of walking." Holmes added: "His face was thin and brown and crafty with a perpetual smile upon it."

Could this be the same man? Could, in a space of 26 years, the 'little weazened man' have become 'small and stout'? Could the 'thin brown face' have become a red face? And could the cringing manner have become a peppery manner?

The answer is patently 'yes, they could'. Over a period of 26 years a thin man can become stout, especially if he drinks, a brown face can become ruddy, again especially if he drinks and a cringing manner, adopted under one set of circumstances, can easily be replaced by a peppery manner if a man has, over the years, acquired a degree of confidence in himself.

Now what of the ages of these two Hudsons? According to the father of Victor Trevor, Hudson had been a 'young seaman' in 1855. Since Trevor at the same time was twenty-three, it is reasonable to assume that Hudson was some years younger, let us say he was about 18.

In 1874, when Holmes was involved, Hudson would have been around thirty-eight, still a youngish man and one who had

W. Wills, Portland Studio, 250 High Road, S. Tottenham.

Inspector Lestrade of Scotland Yard photographed around 1892.

been working hard at sea. If, when he completely disappeared, he had fled to London and taken to a less arduous life than that of a seaman, it is more than likely he would have put on enough weight by the age of sixty-four to be described as 'stout'.

Not conclusive perhaps, but a coincidence nevertheless.

And where does Mrs. Hudson fit in with all this? A relative, a wife, or yet another coincidence?

One can hypothesise that after the *Gloria Scott* affair the young Sherlock Holmes may have met Hudson by chance in London and turned to him on matters relating to the underworld. Since he planned to be a detective, Holmes would have kept in touch. What more natural than when Holmes wanted a new address his friend Hudson, who by now had established himself as a tradesman in south London, should direct him to a female relative? But this is all speculation and as we know 'it is a capital mistake to theorize before you have all the evidence'.

But without theorising we know that Sherlock Holmes was closely associated with a number of police officers. Inspector Lestrade, for example, was involved in no less than thirteen of the sixty cases reported by Watson. The doctor remarked in *The Six Napoleons*; "It was no very unusual thing for Mr. Lestrade to look in upon us of an evening." Holmes, Watson asserted, welcomed Lestrade's visits because 'they enabled him to keep in touch with all that was going on at police headquarters'.

It is no surprise, then, that Lestrade was involved in so many of Holmes's cases. He was giving Holmes information and, no doubt, Holmes acted upon it.

Another detective, Inspector Tobias Gregson, who appeared in four of Watson's accounts, was one of Holmes's earliest Scotland Yard contacts. In January, 1881, he tipped off Holmes about the Lauriston Gardens affair in *A Study in Scarlet*. It was, in fact, Gregson's note asking for 'an opinion' on the case which brought Holmes into it. There was no other client. Yet Holmes did not work for nothing and Gregson certainly would not have had the funds to pay him. But Holmes, who was by no means rich at this time, seemed perfectly happy to take cabs all over London, pay his Baker Street Irregulars and even slip a half-sovereign to a police constable in exchange for information.

If Holmes was not going to make any money from the affair, he must have been after something else. It certainly was not the publicity, since the credit went to the official force. Most likely he was helping Gregson in exchange for information on other matters. It could not have been the normal *quid pro quo* arrangement since Holmes, although he described Gregson as the smartest of Scotland Yarders, would not have wanted help in detection from the Inspector. But Gregson would have had ready access to information that might have been useful to Holmes.

Stanley Hopkins, later in Holmes's career, seemed more closely bound to Holmes than any other detective mentioned in Watson's reports. In 1897, in *The Abbey Grange*, it was a letter from Hopkins, advising Holmes that the affair was in Holmes's 'line', that brought Sherlock Holmes and Watson into the case. There is no other interpretation of Hopkins's letter than that he was advising Holmes that here was a case of murder involving wealthy people and that there might be something to be made out of it. There was clearly no mystery about the affair being worthy of Sherlock Holmes's powers, as we shall see later. Significantly, Hopkins, who was involved in four cases reported by Watson and a further four that were referred to, but never written, abruptly dropped out of sight after this. It is likely that his close involvement with Holmes, particularly as indicated by his letter, was considered prejudicial to the police force and he was transferred to other duties.

Perhaps the most telling incident was that of Police Constable John Rance. He gave some information to Holmes in *A Study in Scarlet* and, in exchange, Sherlock Holmes handed him a half-sovereign.

CHAPTER FIVE

The Seeds of Failure

In April, 1887, Dr. Watson received a telegram telling him that Sherlock Holmes was lying seriously ill in the Hotel Dulong at Lyons. He had collapsed from overwork following his investigations into the Netherland-Sumatra Company and 'the colossal schemes of Baron Maupertuis'[1].

Watson dashed to France to find Holmes suffering from depression and nervous prostration. His 'iron constitution' had broken down under the strain of an investigation which had extended over two months and during which Holmes had worked at least fifteen hours each day. More than once, he told the doctor, he had worked for five days at a stretch.

The success that Holmes had achieved - his hotel room was 'ankle deep in congratulatory telegrams' - was not enough to save him from a reaction to 'so terrible an exertion'.

The doctor was relieved to discover, however, 'there was nothing formidable in his symptoms'. But, as Watson pointed out, "It was to be some time before the health of my friend, Mr. Sherlock Holmes, recovered from the strain". He took Holmes back to Baker Street and then, deciding a short holiday was required, they went to Reigate to visit an old friend of Watson's.

Whether or not the break did Holmes any good we can only guess, but it was about this time that he became a self-poisoner by cocaine[2]. Holmes had experimented with drugs in his youth,

1) *The Reigate Squires*.
2) During their early association Watson had dismissed a suspicion that Holmes was addicted to the use of some narcotic, but for many years Holmes was a user of cocaine. Occasionally he also used morphine. Both drugs were freely available in Victorian London.

leading to his premature departure from Oxford, and there had been some later hints that all was not well in this direction.

Watson, shortly after he and Holmes moved into Baker Street, had suspected something of the sort. He had noticed 'such a dreamy, vacant expression in his eyes, that I might have suspected him of being addicted to some narcotic, had not the temperance and cleanliness of his whole life forbidden such a notion.' With hindsight, of course, we know that such an idea was not out of the question at all. Sherlock Holmes eventually became addicted and quite open about his addiction. In later years Watson was able to wean him off the drug, but the doctor always knew 'that the fiend was not dead, but sleeping'.

Holmes became dependent on cocaine about April, 1887, just after Watson brought him back from France. His huge workload had taken its toll. His health broke down and he sought solace in drugs. A month later Watson, who had married in 1886, and was therefore not living in Baker Street, said that Holmes was 'alternating from week to week between cocaine and ambition'.

The drug addiction and the breakdown affected Holmes's performance for the rest of the year. We have few details of most of his cases in 1887. The Paradol Chamber affair remains a mystery, as does the Amateur Mendicant, the loss of the *Sophy Anderson*, the adventure of the Grice Patersons in the Island of Uffa, the Camberwell poisoning case, the death of Mrs. Lauder and the case of Bert Stevens, the terrible murderer.

The unscrupulous behaviour of Holmes in *A Scandal in Bohemia* has already been demonstrated and in the June of 1887 he was involved in the case of *The Man with the Twisted Lip*. In this, Dr. Watson was consulted by Kate Whitney, a friend of his wife's. Mrs. Whitney called in the late evening of Saturday, 18th June. Her husband Isa Whitney, brother of the late Elias Whitney, D.D., principal of the Theological College of St. George's, was, as Watson asserted, much addicted to opium. It had grown on him when he was at college and for many years he had been 'a slave to the drug'. Watson may well have been thinking of his friend Sherlock Holmes when he wrote of Whitney: "He found, as many more have done, that the practice (of taking drugs) is easier to attain than to get rid of."

Kate Whitney wanted Dr. Watson's advice. Her husband had not been home in two days and she was frightened for him. Watson's wife was also somewhat confused at this point for she referred to her own husband as 'James' rather than as 'John'. Mrs. Whitney told Watson of an opium den[3] used by Whitney where she was sure he was to be found.

Watson set off immediately in a hansom and without difficulty located both the opium den and Isa Whitney. As he was leaving, who should he see but his friend Sherlock Holmes. Sending Whitney home in a cab, Watson stayed to talk with Holmes, who explained he was on a case and 'looking for an enemy' in the opium den. He made a joke of it. "I suppose Watson, that you imagine that I have added opium smoking to cocaine injections and all the other little weaknesses on which you have favoured me with your medical views."

What Holmes, in fact, was doing was investigating the disappearance of one Neville St. Clair, a well-to-do City businessman who, it turned out, made his living from begging in the guise of a man with a twisted lip.

Holmes dealt with all this effectively, but his next recorded case was a different matter. On Thursday, 29th September, he was visited by John Openshaw, a man whose father and uncle had both died after receiving a communication signed K.K.K. and containing five dried orange pips. Openshaw was now rather concerned since he too had received a note from K.K.K. and the five pips. Holmes listened to Openshaw's story, noting that the uncle, the first to die, received an envelope postmarked Pondicherry, the second letter came from Dundee and the third from east London.

He was aware of the danger and told Openshaw: "You must act, man, or you are lost. Nothing but energy can save you." And

---

3) Opium dens were legal and common in London at this time.

later in the same conversation he said: "The first consideration is to remove the pressing danger which threatens you ..."

And then: "The streets will be crowded, so I trust that you may be in safety. And yet you cannot guard yourself too closely."

Holmes was aware that the envelopes containing the pips came from the Ku Klux Klan[4], a 'terrible secret society' which used its power for political purposes, 'murdering or driving from the country' those opposed to its views.

And Holmes could see from the postmarks that the threat was getting nearer. The latest came from London 'and therefore we cannot count upon delay'.

John Openshaw was in immediate and real danger of his life. But what did Holmes do? He railed at the police for 'incredible imbecility' in not realising the danger, he warned Openshaw of his peril and told him he must not 'lose an instant' in taking the action that the Ku Klux Klan wanted, that is, the return of some documents.

But aside from that he put off any action. "Tomorrow I shall set to work upon your case," he told Openshaw. He did not take the young man to a place of safety, or even let him stay at Baker Street. He did not send Watson with him as a bodyguard or go himself. He was confident that, despite the pressing danger and the need for immediate action, it would be alright for him to start work on the case the following day.

Instead of protecting Openshaw, he took up his violin in a bid 'to forget for half an hour the miserable weather, and the still more miserable ways of our fellow-men'.

Openshaw was probably dead before Holmes had finished playing. The morning papers revealed that 'between nine and ten last night' a constable on duty near Waterloo Bridge heard a cry

---

4) The Ku Klux Klan was founded in the U.S.A. about 1866. It declared its purpose as social improvement, but its political purpose was to intimidate negroes and those who favoured the Government's reconstruction measures and prevent them from voting. The KKK committed many outrages and the Government took active measures against the organisation in 1871. However the Klan continued to flourish.

for help and a splash in the water. The body of John Openshaw was eventually recovered and although there were no signs of violence it was clear that Openshaw had fallen victim to the secret society as he went home after meeting Holmes and Watson.

Holmes was 'more depressed and shaken' than Watson had ever seen him. "That hurts my pride," he said. His blunder, and blunder is the kindest word for it since he allowed his client to roam around London with a gang of killers at his heels, to all intents and purposes marks the end of the case.

Certainly Holmes claimed to have identified the killers. His evidence seems to be that a particular ship was berthed in each of the ports from which one of the K.K.K. letters was posted at the time it was sent. However, this appears to be the full extent of the case against his suspects and it may well be that Sherlock Holmes was acting a little prematurely in writing to the chief of police at the ship's next port of call advising him that certain members of the crew were 'badly wanted' in London on a murder charge. However, this is all somewhat hypothetical. Holmes may well have been able to produce conclusive evidence which would have satisfied a court. In any event, the suspects were never charged. Watson tells us their ship disappeared in the Atlantic and they were presumed drowned.

There can be no doubt that John Openshaw's death was due to Holmes's negligence. Had he been doing his job properly, the young man would never have been put in the position where he could be murdered.

But at this time Sherlock Holmes was not doing his job properly. Since his breakdown in the early part of the year and his subsequent addiction to cocaine, Holmes had, on the evidence available, begun to behave quite oddly and the shock of Openshaw's death was to add to the burden he must carry.

We should not assume that *The Five Orange Pips* was the first time Holmes had made a serious mistake, however. He told Openshaw at their meeting that he had been 'beaten four times - three times by men and once by a woman' and Watson was to explain later that it was 'only natural that I should dwell upon his successes rather than on failures'.

Failures there certainly were and there seems to have been an accumulation of them towards the end of the 1880s.

Oddities in Holmes's behaviour were first noticed immediately after the Netherland-Sumatra Company investigation. In Reigate, during his visit there with Watson, the local police inspector pointed out that Holmes was not over his illness and was 'behaving very queerly'. He even suggested there was 'madness in his method'.

A month after returning from Reigate, Holmes was acting very questionably in *A Scandal in Bohemia*. The death of John Openshaw followed later in the year.

That case and its serious consequences may have given Holmes pause for thought. He may even have temporarily given up the drug which was threatening permanently to harm his career. There is certainly no mention of his addiction for the rest of the year and the four cases handled by Holmes in that period were dealt with effectively. *A Case of Identity* was of minor importance and Holmes did not leave Baker Street to establish that it was Miss Mary Sutherland's stepfather James Windibank who had disguised himself as Mr. Hosmer Angel, proposed marriage to Miss Sutherland, and then jilted her. His motive had been to ensure that Miss Sutherland never married and that her small income continued to benefit the family home.

The Red Headed League at the end of October ended in the arrest of the notorious John Clay whom Holmes described as a villain 'at the head of his profession'. Inspector Peter Jones said that he would rather have his 'bracelets on him than on any criminal in London'. Clearly young Mr. Clay, a murderer, thief, smasher and forger, grandson of a royal duke and product of Eton and Oxford, was a criminal mastermind of the first order. His brain, according to Inspector Jones, was 'as cunning as his fingers' and he admitted that the police saw signs of Clay at every turn, but never knew where to find the man himself. The arrest was quite a coup for Holmes.

But again trouble loomed. In November, 1887, Sherlock Holmes found himself up against the formidable Culverton Smith, the murderer of Victor Savage, and in *The Dying Detective* Holmes successfully set a trap to wring an admission of guilt from the killer. But in doing so he feigned illness, taking neither food nor drink for three days to make it convincing.

This abuse of his body was to take an even greater toll than Holmes or Watson suspected.

It would be a month before Holmes could take on another case. This was the somewhat whimsical affair of *The Blue Carbuncle*. Watson had called on his friend on the second morning after Christmas to find him studying a disreputable hard felt hat which hung from the back of a chair. The hat eventually led to the discovery of the Countess of Morcar's missing blue carbuncle, a jewel worth more than £20,000. Holmes took no action against the thief. After all, it was, as he pointed out to Watson 'the season of forgiveness'.

The year ended happily enough. Watson no doubt was under the impression that Holmes had finally recovered from the terrible exertion of the Netherland-Sumatra Company case. He had been successful and seemed to be back to normal.

It was, however, only a temporary respite.

Mrs Hudson, landlady of 221B Baker Street.

CHAPTER SIX

The Crooked Professor

The first hint that there was trouble at Birlstone Manor in Sussex came from Sherlock Holmes's informant, Fred Porlock. But by the time his warning arrived in Baker Street and had been decoded it was too late - a man was dead.

The supposed victim was Mr. John Douglas, but as Holmes was to discover, Douglas was still very much alive. The corpse, with the face destroyed by a blast from a double-barrelled shotgun, was in fact that of Ted Baldwin, who had pursued Douglas from the coalfields of Pennsylvania to kill him. The gun had gone off as the two men struggled, killing Baldwin and rendering his body unrecognisable.

Douglas, who was being pursued by the Scowrers, a 'gang of murderers' from the Vermissa Valley[1], saw his chance to end their persecution. Aided by a friend, he dressed the body in his own clothes, put a plaster on its chin to correspond with one on his own, and went into hiding. Holmes was not fooled, however, and eventually got at the truth.

In the ensuing court case Douglas was acquitted of the murder of Baldwin, the jury accepting his plea that he acted in self defence. Holmes told Douglas's wife: "Get him out of England at any cost. There are forces here which may be more dangerous than those he has escaped."

The warning was in vain. Two months later an enigmatic note was slipped through the Baker Street letter box. "Dear me! Mr.

---

1) A coal mining area of the United States located in the Gilmerton Mountains. The main town is Vermissa.

Holmes! Dear me!" it read. Later that day the news came that Douglas, who, together with his wife, had taken a ship for South Africa, was dead. He had been mysteriously lost overboard in a gale off St Helena. Douglas's friend who brought the news to Baker Street believed the Scowrers to be responsible.

Holmes, however, regarded things differently. The Scowrers, a 'vindictive nest of criminals' were not, in the final analysis, responsible for the death of Douglas. They may have chased him across the world with the intention of killing him, but after Ted Baldwin was shot dead, another, more powerful, organisation took a hand. "I can tell a Moriarty when I see one," said Holmes. He was referring to Professor James Moriarty, distinguished scientist and author of *The Dynamics of an Asteroid*, a man whose name had resounded across Europe after the publication of his treatise on the binomial theorem[2].

Sherlock Holmes was of the view that the Professor was a criminal mastermind, the controlling brain of the underworld. But how could he have had anything to do with the murder of Douglas? It was the killing of an American, ordered by an American organisation in revenge for events in the American coalfields. The Scowrers had already sent one killer after him, so why should they not send another?

"I can only say that the first word that ever came to us of the business was from one of [Moriarty's] lieutenants," said Holmes, referring to Porlock's warning. He speculated that having 'an English job' to do, the Scowrers took into partnership, as any foreign criminal could, 'this great consultant of crime'. Holmes continued: "From that moment their man was doomed, At first [Moriarty] would content himself by using his machinery in order to find their victim. Then he would indicate how the matter might be treated. Finally, when he read in the reports of the failure of

---

2)   A mathematical theorem devised by Newton for raising a binomial (two terms connected by + or -) to any power, or for extracting the root of it by an approximately infinite series.

this agent, he would step in himself with the master touch."

Moriarty's motive for getting involved? According to Holmes: "It is done by a man who cannot afford to fail ... It is crushing the nut with the hammer ... but the nut is very effectively crushed all the same."

Early in 1888 Sherlock Holmes believed that Professor Moriarty was 'the greatest schemer of all time, the organizer of every devilry, the controlling brain of the underworld'.

Yet this master criminal had come on to the scene rather suddenly. In October, 1887, at the time of *The Red Headed League*, Holmes had been unaware of his existence. It is unthinkable that if he had known of the Professor's alleged activities he would have referred to John Clay as being 'at the head of his profession'. That was a position occupied by Professor Moriarty. Equally, Scotland Yard had heard nothing to the detriment of the Professor. "We in the CID think that you have a wee bit of a bee in your bonnet over this Professor," said Inspector MacDonald in *The Valley of Fear*.

Is it possible that the Professor had recently arrived in London and become the underworld's 'controlling brain'? Clearly it is not. Holmes claimed that Moriarty's organisation carried out the murder of John Douglas, acting as 'consultant' to the Scowrers, That kind of international criminal reputation takes a long time to build up. In that case the Professor must have been around for some time.

However, it is equally unlikely that the Professor could have been operating in London without at least some hint of his activities reaching Sherlock Holmes and Scotland Yard. He could not control the underworld if he was completely anonymous and he could not act as a consultant in crime if no-one had ever heard of him. If he was known to the criminal classes, he would have been known to Holmes and the Yard. The Scowrers were able to make contact with Moriarty's organisation, according to Holmes, and therefore Moriarty was also known overseas.

Moriarty was not controlling the underworld on 29th October, 1887, when Holmes investigated the John Clay case. If he had been, then Sherlock Holmes and Scotland Yard would have been aware of it, even if they did not have enough evidence to bring charges against him.

But Moriarty would have been unable simply to turn up and take control in the couple of months before *The Valley of Fear*.

Therefore at first sight it would appear to be impossible that Professor Moriarty was in control of the underworld at any time.

In that case, where had the notion that he was an arch-criminal come from? The answer is shown in the first chapter of *The Valley of Fear*: Fred Porlock. He is the key to the whole Moriarty mystery.

But who was Fred Porlock? The name, he had told Sherlock Holmes in an earlier letter, was false, and he had defied Holmes ever to trace him, In fact Holmes knew practically nothing about his informant, "Porlock," he said, "is important not for himself, but for the great man with whom he is in touch," Holmes had paid Porlock for his information, but had sent the money 'in notes to Camberwell post-office'. He had never troubled to see who called for them because, as he told Inspector MacDonald, "I always keep faith. I had promised when he first wrote that I would not try to trace him."

There is no doubt that the first indication that Professor Moriarty was engaged in illegal activities came, as far as Holmes was concerned, in a note from Porlock. But was there corroboration from other sources? In short, despite Holmes's efforts, the answer is no. He had not managed to uncover any other evidence against the Professor.

"I have been three times in his rooms," said Holmes. The first two occasions he waited for the Professor on different pretexts, but left before he arrived. The third time "I took the liberty of running over his papers, with the most unexpected results".

Inspector MacDonald pricked up his ears: "You found

something compromising?"

"Absolutely nothing," admitted Holmes. "That was what amazed me." He was amazed because he had expected to discover incriminating evidence, but if Moriarty was nothing more than he appeared, that is, a brilliant mathematician, then it is hardly surprising he had nothing compromising in his belongings.

Holmes could bring only one fact to support his contention that Moriarty was a master criminal, Despite having a salary of only seven hundred pounds a year, he had managed to become the owner of a painting by Greuze[3] which fetched 'not less than four thousand pounds' when it was sold in 1865.

Holmes did not even consider the possibility of inherited wealth or that he could have in any way obtained it honestly. Yet while we must accept that Moriarty owned this painting, Holmes did not suggest that the Professor owned any other objects of great value and he would have certainly mentioned it if he had.

The police did not support Holmes's view of Professor Moriarty. Inspector MacDonald thought the Professor "seems to be a very respectable, learned and talented sort of man". He had, at Holmes' urging, made some inquiries about Moriarty, but had failed to discover anything against him.

The situation with regard to James Moriarty was this: Fred Porlock said he was a master criminal and Sherlock Holmes believed him. Yet if Porlock's story was true, Holmes would have heard of Moriarty, the master criminal. On top of this, when Holmes and MacDonald made inquiries about the Professor, neither came up with anything that could be held against him.

The weight of the evidence certainly indicates that Moriarty was nothing more than he appeared on the surface: a brilliant mathematician earning seven hundred pounds a year who owned one expensive painting.

---

3)   Jean Baptiste Greuze (1725-1805). A French painter whose work represents a sentimental return to nature.

Nevertheless, Sherlock Holmes remained totally convinced by Fred Porlock's story, He admitted, however, that Porlock was the only source of information he had about the Professor. Porlock, said Holmes, 'is a link in the chain some little way from its great attachment'.

However, the message which Porlock sent to Holmes at the beginning of *The Valley of Fear* should be enough to establish his credibility once and for all. When decoded it read: "There is danger - may come very soon one Douglas - rich country - now at Birlstone House Birlstone - confidence is pressing".

This was a clear warning that there was pressing danger for someone called Douglas who was posing as a rich country gentleman and living at Birlstone House.

Soon after Holmes and Watson read the message, Inspector MacDonald called: John Douglas, he said, was shot dead the previous night at Birlstone Manor, in Sussex.

This would appear to be enough to satisfy even the most sceptical that Porlock was privy to criminal secrets and therefore should be listened to when he spoke of Professor Moriarty. He had, after all, had foreknowledge of a murder and had put his warning in writing to Sherlock Holmes ... or had he?

If we continue to accept that the great weight of evidence was against Moriarty being a master criminal, then it must be assumed that Porlock was telling lies about him. Were he lying about that, then he must be lying about this murder. Yet the murder had happened just as Porlock warned it would. There-fore, how could anyone say he did not know it was going to occur?

The answer lies in the timing of the killing and the writing of the note. The shooting took place at about 10.45 p.m. on Friday, 6th January. At 11.15 p.m., after a cover-up had been arranged, the alarm was raised. A message reached the local police station at 11.45 p.m. and the police got to Birlstone a little after midnight. By that time the county authorities had been warned that a serious crime had been committed. The local detective officer, White Mason, had sent a message to Inspector MacDonald at Scotland Yard in the early hours of the morning, asking him to go down to Birlstone to assist.

Messages about the crime were being sent between Birlstone Manor, the local police station, county headquarters and Scotland Yard from midnight onwards. No-one was trying to keep the killing secret and dozens of people would have known about it. It was too late for the morning newspapers, but it may well have been known in newspaper offices by the early hours of the morning[4]. White Mason's message to Inspector MacDonald arrived at Scotland Yard probably by a little before 6.00 a.m. He had been to the scene of the crime and carried out a preliminary investigation before contacting his colleague in London. But the county authorities had known early on that Mr. Douglas of Birlstone Manor had been shot and would have alerted the Yard without waiting for Mason's preliminary inquiry.

Sherlock Holmes was studying the coded message from Porlock at about 10.00 a.m. on Saturday, 7th January. His breakfast was untouched and Watson was up and about. The second post arrived a few minutes later with a second note from Porlock.

We must remember that the cipher had arrived in an envelope unaccompanied by any key. Holmes was expecting the key to arrive in the second post. However, the second communication from Porlock said simply that it was too dangerous for him to continue and he begged Holmes to destroy the coded message "which can now be of no use ..."

Holmes was, of course, able to decipher the message fairly easily. He explained to Watson that the reason for putting the cipher and the key in separate envelopes was that if either went astray it would, on its own, be meaningless.

The point about the hours which elapsed between the shooting

---

[4] In fact the last editions of the morning papers were printed around 2 a.m. and had the editors considered the story merited coverage, the item could have appeared that morning.

61

and Holmes receiving the cipher is that since a fairly large number of people were aware in the early hours of the morning that the crime had been committed, it would have been perfectly feasible for one of those people, if he was really Porlock, to write the warning and put it into code.

Thus the 'warning' could have been written after the crime was committed, giving the impression that Porlock had known in advance what was going to happen. The difficulty with this theory is that although the cipher could have been written in the time available, it would have been touch and go whether it would have caught the post in time to be included in the first delivery at Baker Street.

The letter from Porlock saying it was too dangerous for him to continue giving information arrived in the second post. That we have from Watson as a fact. But since the cipher had arrived earlier and was waiting for Holmes on the breakfast table, we are led to assume it arrived in the first postal delivery.

But is it certain that it was posted at all? When Holmes opened it he examined both paper and envelope, but made no mention of any postmark. There was, in fact, no suggestion that Porlock's message had been sent through the post. It is just as likely that it was delivered by hand.

There was no problem with the letter which arrived in the second post. It bore a Camberwell postmark and, in 1888, if it had been posted by 8.00 a.m. in that district of London it would have reached Baker Street with the second delivery.

Consequently we see that the anonymous Fred Porlock would have had the opportunity to learn that there had been a shooting, write a coded warning and send it round to Baker Street in time for Holmes to open it as he sat down to his late breakfast. Porlock would also have been able to write his letter telling Holmes to forget the whole thing, post it in Camberwell, and be confident that it would arrive in the second delivery.

It is possible, then, that Porlock did not have advance

knowledge that an attempt was to be made on John Douglas's life. But in that event we must conclude he was deliberately trying to mislead Sherlock Holmes.

Therefore we must echo Watson: "Who, then, is Porlock?"

To have written the coded note after the shooting means that Porlock must have learned of the shooting before about 7.00 a.m. This limit was to give him time to get the second letter posted so that it was delivered in Baker Street at about 10.00 a.m. Now who knew about the shooting within the time limits?

There are three distinct groups of people who were aware the shooting had taken place. There was the Douglas household, police officers in Sussex and London, and finally post office employees who may have transmitted or delivered telegrams.

Now, if Porlock was attempting to mislead Holmes, it implies that he had some previous contact with him. Of the three groups that knew the crime had occurred, Holmes had most contact with police officers, and specifically with Scotland Yard detectives.

Could it be that Fred Porlock was a detective in the Metropolitan Police? A Yard man would certainly have had the opportunity, since the news of the Birlstone shooting would have come in overnight. But what would have been his motive?

Let us examine the effect of playing such a prank on Holmes, of convincing him that one of the leading scientists of the day was the head of a vast criminal organisation. It would have made a fool of Holmes. It would have been quite a chuckle in the detectives' room at the Yard, corresponding with Holmes and building up a picture of the famous scientist as a criminal mastermind, watching Holmes chase here and there trying to get proof of Porlock's allegations.

But why pick on Professor Moriarty as the master criminal? Holmes liked to think of himself as a scientific detective. How amusing it would have seemed to pit him against a scientific criminal. And who would make a better adversary than England's foremost scientist, Professor James Moriarty?

It was just the kind of hoax that a disgruntled detective might play if he thought Holmes was getting a bit above himself, a little too clever for his own good.

And Sherlock Holmes had been reported as making some pretty damaging remarks about Scotland Yard only about a month earlier. *A Study in Scarlet* had been published in December, 1887, and in it Holmes described the motive for a crime as "so transparent that even a Scotland Yard official can see through it".

That, coupled with his arrogant assurance to Watson that when official detectives got into difficulty "they come to me and I manage to put them on the right scent" was hardly calculated to win him any friends at the Yard, especially when it was printed in a mass circulation publication.

Holmes's attitude towards Scotland Yard officers meant that many would have liked a chance to put him in his place. But which officer actually thought out a plan and put it into practice?

The clue is 'Camberwell'. Porlock's letter was postmarked Camberwell and he received his payment at Camberwell post office. He clearly had a connection there. A few months earlier Holmes had solved a poisoning case at Camberwell. Watson did not record the full details, but said in *The Five Orange Pips* that Holmes "was able, by winding up the dead man's watch, to prove that it had been wound up two hours ago, and that the deceased had gone to bed within that time - a deduction which was of the greatest importance in clearing up the case".

This masterly deduction may not have pleased the police officer in charge of the case. He might well have considered that the theorist had shown him up as inadequate, making him the butt of his colleagues' jokes and his superiors' anger.

So who was the detective in charge of the Camberwell poisoning case? The Metropolitan Police at that time, as now, preferred to assign to a case an officer who was familiar with the area in which the crime had taken place. Consequently the detective assigned to the Camberwell poisoning case would probably be a man who had gone to the Yard after service in south east London. He may well have lived in the area.

We have no evidence to show that any detective known to Holmes at about this time had come from Camberwell or the surrounding area. But we do know of one officer who was active in south east London only a few months after the events of *The Valley of Fear*. And he was an officer who was openly hostile to Sherlock Holmes, sneering at the 'theorizer' and recalling how Holmes had 'lectured' the police over the Bishopsgate jewel case.

That man was Mr. Athelney Jones. He took over the inquiry into the tragedy of Pondicherry Lodge in *The Sign of Four* after being 'out at Norwood over another case'. Pondicherry Lodge is also situated in Norwood and Miss Mary Morstan, the young lady in the affair, who was eventually to become Watson's bride, lived with Mrs. Cecil Forrester in nearby Camberwell. Thus in *The Sign of Four* we find Athelney Jones dealing with two cases a short distance from Fred Porlock's home territory of Camberwell.

Jones may have lived in Camberwell which would have made it more convenient for him to deal with cases in the south east area of London But perhaps most significant is his hostility to Holmes The two men had clearly crossed swords at some time in the past. Yet while Holmes was prone to 'lecture' the police, he was not inclined to take the credit for his successes and detectives like Lestrade and Gregson were happy to have him in an investigation, knowing it would be of benefit to them if Holmes came up with an anonymous solution.

But Jones's attitude to Holmes is entirely different. He is contemptuous and unwilling to have him involved.

Eventually, in *The Sign of Four*, Athelney Jones, realising he is out of his depth, comes to Baker Street for help "I should be very glad of a little assistance," he told Watson, for Holmes was out, and the policeman added an eulogy to Sherlock Holmes. "Your friend Mr. Sherlock Holmes is a wonderful man, sir," said Jones. "He's a man not to be beat. I have known that young man

Miss Mary Morstan, who became Mrs Watson in 1889.

go into a good many cases, hut I never saw the case yet that he could not throw a light on."

As Watson pointed out, Mr. Jones's attitude has changed. "Very different was he, however, from the brusque and masterful professor of commonsense who had taken over the case so confidently at Upper Norwood."

Jones makes the reason quite clear. He has arrested the wrong man and has been left looking rather silly. "My professional credit is at stake," he told Watson.

The attitude may have changed, but it all had rather the ring of the bully pleading for mercy when he is beaten. Nevertheless, Holmes was happy to give quarter. "I insist upon your dining with us," he told Jones. "I have oysters and a brace of grouse, with something a little choice in white wines."

The dinner was a success. Watson reported that "Athelney Jones proved to be a sociable soul in his hours of relaxation". Clearly relations were cemented and at the conclusion of the case Holmes allowed Jones to take the credit for bringing the villains to justice.

However, in the earlier Camberwell poisoning case there had been no cementing of relations. Holmes's amazing deduction about the watch had been the critical factor in solving the crime and he had made no secret of it. Athelney Jones had been overcome with resentment and had decided to create the informer 'Fred Porlock', convincing Holmes that Professor Moriarty was an arch-criminal.

Jones was at Scotland Yard on the night that news of the Birlstone shooting came in. He would have spotted an ideal opportunity to make a fool of Sherlock Holmes once more, reinforcing the amateur's belief that Porlock's information was reliable. He would have quickly written his warning and put it into code, the copy of *Whitaker's Almanack* - readily available in the detectives' room - as the key to his cipher, and then sent it round to Baker Street by hand.

Later on he may have felt things had gone a little far. After all, the cipher message, although intended as a joke, was in fact a piece of false evidence that might mislead a murder hunt. If that ever came back to Athelney Jones, it would have had a serious effect on his career. He would have decided that the best thing to do was write to Holmes as Porlock and ask him to burn the cipher. Having written the letter, he would have waited until he was well clear of Scotland Yard before posting it. There was, after all, no urgency. Holmes could do nothing without the key to the code, so it was quite safe for Jones to wait until he got off the omnibus in Camberwell on his way home before posting his letter. After his night stint at the Yard he would have got home at about 7.00 a.m. The letter would have arrived in Baker Street by the second post and Jones would have felt secure in the knowledge that no harm had been done.

But he had underestimated Sherlock Holmes the 'theorizer'. Jones's letter as 'Porlock' simply spurred Holmes to decipher the coded message, convincing him once and for all that Porlock was telling the truth.

Finally, we must deal with the note which at the end of *The Valley of Fear* was pushed through the Baker Street letter box. It read: "Dear me! Mr. Holmes! Dear me!" Watson laughed it off, but Holmes's brow clouded. "Devilry, Watson," he said. It was implied that this note came from Professor Moriarty, crowing over the death, at last, of John Douglas. It obviously had not come from the Professor, but was it yet another fake communication from Athelney Jones?

Unlike the Porlock letter, in this case it cannot be finally established. However, in *The Sign of Four* Jones did show a tendency to repeat a phrase or exclamation: "Bad business! Bad business!" he said. "Don't promise too much, Mr. Theorist, don't promise too much."

Significantly upon learning that jewellery worth half a million pounds was missing, Jones showed that he was in the habit of using the expression 'dear me!'

But this can hardly be conclusive. Watson was probably quite right to dismiss the note as irrelevant. It was, after all, most likely the work of a crank or eccentric who had recently finished reading of Holmes in *Beeton's Christmas Annual*. It is, however, just possibile that the practical joker, Athelney Jones, had written it, his courage restored once the Douglas case was complete.

The 'dear me!' note was to have no effect on the final result of Athelney Jones's hoax. From the moment Sherlock Holmes received the cipher which 'warned' of the attempt to kill John Douglas, he was completely convinced that Moriarty was a criminal mastermind who controlled the underworld.

From then on the innocent Professor of mathematics was doomed.

Professor James Moriarty, pictured in 1886.

S. GREY
PHOTOGRAPHER
144 Western Road
BRIGHTON

CHAPTER SEVEN

The Curious Incident of Sherlock Holmes
and the Whitechapel Murders

In the year 1888, Victoria was Queen of England, Lord Salisbury her Prime Minister, and Grover Cleveland the President of the United States. London, with a population exceeding six and a half million people, was the largest city in the world. In Whitehall, the Government controlled the greatest empire the world had known. In the financial district, bankers ruled a monetary domain which spanned the globe. In the docks, cargoes were despatched and received from every corner of the earth; and in London's East End, Jack the Ripper unleashed a reign of terror.

The one man who could have revealed the killer sat in Baker Street, haunted by fears of madness. Sherlock Holmes, racked by months of failure, drug addiction and self-doubt, believed he had become, in his own words, 'a lunatic, a man with softening of the brain, an idiot whose mind has lost its grip.'[1]

The murders had started on 31st August, when the body of Mary Ann Nichols, a 42 year old prostitute, was found in Bucks Row, a dimly-lit street in Whitechapel. She had been horrifically mutilated; her throat had been cut so deeply that the spinal cord was severed and there were massive injuries to the abdomen.

The body was noticed at about 3.40 a.m. by a man on his way to work who called the police. She was lying in the entrance to some stables, less than thirty feet from the nearest houses. The killer had been able to seize his victim, force her to the ground and carry out his frenzied attack within sight and sound of the nearby households and then leave the area unseen. It was this swift, silent, murderous technique which sent the first shudders

1) *The Valley of Fear.*

of panic through the people of the East End.

Four more women were to die before the nightmare was over. All were prostitutes who worked the streets of Whitechapel charging each client a few pence. All were savagely mutilated. Annie Chapman was murdered in Hanbury Street on 8th September; Elizabeth Stride in Berner Street and Catharine Eddowes in Mitre Square, both on 30th September; and Mary Jane Kelly was killed in her room in Dorset Street on 9th November. After the last murder, the killer disappeared completely. He was never caught; he was never identified.

The first two murders created an immediate sensation. The sheer savagery of the attacks sent a wave of horror through London. Police flooded Whitechapel in the hunt for the killer. Newspapermen interviewed and questioned anyone who would help them compile lurid reports of the attacks and wild theories about the identity of the murderer. And then, on 28th September, just as the panic was beginning to subside and the story was dying, a letter to the Central News Agency in Fleet Street caused a new sensation. It provided the name by which the killer would forever be known. It threatened more murders and was signed *'Jack the Ripper'*.

Jack the Ripper was not the first multiple murderer. Nor was he the first sex murderer. He was, however, the first serial sex killer to be the subject of massive publicity, the first to be the subject of a massive police hunt, and the first to create a climate of terror through his apparently random outrages. The combined resources of the Metropolitan Police and the City of London force[2] failed to unmask him and a posse of amateur detectives, both at the time and subsequently, have been unable to identify the murderer.

There have, of course, been suspects. Detectives had their suspicions in 1888, and, until the present day, writers have

2) The Metropolitan Police had and have jurisdiction in the entire Greater London area with the exception of the square mile centred on the Bank of England, which is the responsibility of the City of London force.

levelled accusations against a myriad of notable and obscure Victorians. In each case, the argument has failed through lack of convincing evidence.

Most notable among these suspects was the Duke of Clarence, a grandson of Queen Victoria, who would have succeeded his father, Edward VII, as King of England had he not died in 1892 of pneumonia. The Duke was accused of the Jack the Ripper murders in an article published in 1970 in *The Criminologist* magazine by Dr Thomas Stowell. He based his charge on papers left by the Queen's physician, Sir William Gull.

Subsequent research, however, established that Clarence had been at Sandringham in Norfolk on the night of the Kelly murder, and when Stride and Eddowes were killed he was several hundred miles away, at Balmoral in Scotland.

Sir William Gull himself was named as the Ripper in a BBC television series in 1974. This came to the conclusion that Gull, a royal coachman, John Netley, and the famous painter Walter Sickert were engaged in a conspiracy to silence the victims because they were attempting to blackmail the royal family. The theory was that the Duke of Clarence had fathered an illegitimate child by an Irish Catholic woman, an act which could have endangered the British Crown.

The source of this was Joseph Sickert, the son of the painter and in the last episode of the series he elaborated on his allegations. In 1976 the Gull-Netley-Sickert theory appeared in a book by Stephen Knight, *Jack the Ripper - the Final Solution*, which added in elements of freemasonry and involvement by the Government in the cover-up and the conspiracy. But other investigators were already having serious doubts about the story. It had been established that Gull was an invalid at the time of the murders, having suffered a serious stroke the previous year which had left him paralysed and therefore unlikely to be physically capable of carrying out the crimes even with help. Finally, Joseph Sickert confessed. In 1978 he told the London *Sunday Times* that he had made up the whole thing. "It was a hoax," he said. "A whopping fib."

Tricksters and conmen are one hazard in the continuing hunt for the identity of Jack the Ripper, but there are also the traps of wishful thinking and pure fantasy on the part of the investigators. Thus, there have been attempts to incriminate a Russian doctor, a black magician, a Tsarist agent sent to cause chaos in London, a friend of Oscar Wilde and a mad midwife.

More serious researchers have considered a young barrister, Montague Druitt, a likely candidate. He, like the Duke of Clarence, who he closely resembled, fitted the description of a man seen by witnesses in the company of several of the Ripper's victims shortly before their bodies were found; he had some links with the East End; and he committed suicide soon after the last murder. He came to the attention of the police after his body was found in the Thames and was investigated, like countless others, as a possible suspect, but there was not a shred of evidence against him

Later writers have investigated Druitt because he was named as having been the subject of police inquiries by Sir Melville Macnaghten, who became Assistant Commissioner and head of the Criminal Investigation Department at Scotland Yard in 1903. Much has been made of Macnaghten's notes on the crimes, but his connection with them is slight; in fact, he did not join Scotland Yard until six months after the last of the murders. He became involved some six years later when a report in *The Sun* newspaper claimed to have identified the Ripper as a man named Thomas Cutbush.

Cutbush was a nephew of a former police superintendent and, in an effort to refute the allegation, which carried the implication that the police had known the perpetrator all along and done nothing because of his uncle's connections, Macnaghten set down what he knew of the murders in a series of notes. He stated: "Many homicidal maniacs were suspected, but no shadow of proof could be thrown on any one," and he went on to list three men, "any one of whom would have been more likely than

Cutbush to have committed this series of murders".

The three were Druitt; a Polish jew called Kosminski; and a Russian doctor, Michael Ostrog, who was never traced. It should be noted that Macnaghten did not say any of these were likely to be the Ripper, just that they were more likely than Cutbush.

Because he had no direct link with the case and because of the passage of time, Macnaghten's testimony must be viewed as, at best, unreliable, but other police officers were in a better position to give an opinion.

Four of the five murders came within the jurisdiction of the Metropolitan Police and were therefore investigated by Scotland Yard. Catharine Eddowes was killed in Mitre Square in Aldgate and so that killing fell to the City of London force to investigate.

The Metropolitan Police Commissioner during the Ripper murders was Sir Charles Warren. He resigned in November, 1888, immediately after the final atrocity and was succeeded by James Munro, a former head of the Criminal Investigation Department. So during the period in question Scotland Yard was led by two men. The Commissioner of the City police was Sir James Fraser.

These three , more than anyone else, were ideally placed to know in what direction the evidence pointed. If there was a suspect, even if there was insufficient evidence to support a charge, they would have known. Unfortunately they took that knowledge to the grave; none published memoirs and no papers have been discovered in which they expressed an opinion.

Two men who were closely involved in the hunt for the Ripper left memoirs. They were Major Henry Smith, the Chief Superintendent of the City police, who, because of the Commissioner's impending retirement, had complete charge of the Eddowes investigation; and Robert Anderson, who was Assistant Commissioner at Scotland Yard and head of the Criminal Investigation Department from the summer of 1888 until his retirement in 1901. He was, therefore, in command of the hunt for the Ripper throughout.

Sir Charles Warren, Commissioner of the Metropolitan Police at the time of the hunt for Jack the Ripper.

We can learn little from Henry Smith's book, published in 1910. In it he boasted, "There is no man living who knows as much of those murders as I do", but he was forced to admit that he had no idea about the killer's identity.

Anderson's memoirs, however, are a different matter. In 1907 he published *Criminals and Crime: Some Facts and Suggestions* in which he stated that the Ripper was 'safely caged in an asylum' and three years later, in *The Lighter Side of my Official Life*, he said unequivocally that he knew the identity of Jack the Ripper. He wrote: "I am almost tempted to disclose the identity of the murderer ... but no public benefit would result from such a course." He went on to explain the reason for his certainty on the matter, "the only person who ever had a good view of the murderer at once identified him".

So why not prosecute? There are two reasons: we can infer that since the killer was 'caged in an asylum' he had been judged mad; and Anderson states that, having carried out the identification, the witness refused to testify.

This is tantalising, but ultimately unsatisfactory. The man at the head of the investigation claimed to know the identity of the Ripper and asserted that a positive identification was made, but, coyly, declined to name the suspect. Fortunately another senior policeman was less reticent.

In the autumn of 1888 Chief Inspector Donald Swanson was appointed to co-ordinate the hunt for the Ripper. He was given a special office at Scotland Yard to process all the papers on the Whitechapel murders and he prepared regular reports on the progress of the investigation for the Commissioner, Anderson and the Home Secretary. This put him in the unique position of being the only man to see every report, every piece of evidence and every statement relating to the crimes.

Swanson never published his memoirs, but his thoughts on Jack the Ripper still survive. In his copy of Anderson's second book, discovered among his effects after his death, Swanson pencilled some notes and signed his initials beside them. In the margin, where Anderson asserted the Ripper had been identified, Swanson wrote: "After this identification which the suspect knew, no other murders of this kind took place in London." And on the endpaper there is another note in which Swanson said the identification took place at 'the seaside home'. He then gave the name of the man he believed to be Jack the Ripper: *Kosminski was the suspect - DSS.*

So now we have it, backed by the authority of Robert Anderson who commanded Scotland Yard's Criminal Investigation Department, and Chief Inspector Swanson who co-ordinated the inquiry. The name of the man, positively identified as the Whitechapel murderer, was Kosminski.

Now, of course, there are other questions: Who was Kosminski? What did he look like? What eventually happened to him? Who identified him? And why did he refuse to testify against him?

Swanson answered two of those questions and provided a clue which makes it possible to solve one other. Anderson's book said that the suspect, Kosminski, was a Polish Jew. Swanson's pencilled notes add that the witness who identified him was also Jewish and he refused to testify against a fellow Jew "and also because his evidence would convict the suspect, and witness would be the means of the murderer being hanged which he did not wish to be left on his mind".

As to Kosminski's eventual fate, Swanson says: "On suspect's return to his brother's house in Whitechapel, he was watched by police [City CID] by day and night. In a very short time the suspect, with his hands tied behind his back, was sent to Stepney Workhouse and then to Colney Hatch and died shortly afterwards."

Colney Hatch was an asylum outside London and is, therefore, the place where Anderson considered the Ripper to be 'safely caged'.

To discover what Kosminski looked like, it is necessary to discover the witness at the 'seaside home'. This phrase had only one meaning to police officers at the time; it referred to a convalescent home at Bexhill in Kent on the south coast of England. The Convalescent Home Fund had been established in 1887 and policemen were sent there for recuperation throughout 1888. If the identification took place there, as Swanson asserted, it could only mean that the witness was a police officer.

Among the mass of evidence which the investigating teams accumulated, there were a number of statements from witnesses who had seen the victims in the company of men shortly before their deaths. More than half these statements contain descriptions with enough common points to indicate the witnesses had all seen the same man. They were describing Jack the Ripper.

Two of these witnesses were policemen. One, Detective Sergeant Stephen White, had a close view of the killer and was able to give a detailed description of him. White's description of the suspected murderer was widely circulated and in 1919 his account of his brush with Jack the Ripper was published in *The Peoples' Journal*.

On the night of the murder of Elizabeth Stride, White was watching an alley just behind the Whitechapel Road. He said there was only one way in and one way out and the police had two officers keeping it under observation. As White approached to get a report from the constables, a well-dressed man emerged from the alley, wished him goodnight and exchanged comments about the weather. The police immediately went into the alley and found the body of Stride. The man had disappeared into the crowd by this time, but White had seen him clearly under a street light. He said the suspect was about five feet ten inches tall; aged about thirty-three; shabby, but in clothes of good material; his face was long and thin; his hair was jet black; his complexion was sallow; his eyes were extraordinarily brilliant; his hands were snow white; his fingers long and tapering; and his voice was cultured and musical.

This is, by far, the most detailed description of a Jack the Ripper suspect and it was consistent with the less-complete testimony of other witnesses. Constable William Smith, the second police officer to provide a description, saw a man of medium height, about twenty eight years old, he thought, dressed in a dark-coloured coat and deerstalker hat with Elizabeth Stride shortly before her body was found.

A man seen by a Mrs Elizabeth Long with Annie Chapman on the night of her murder was described as being of shabby, genteel appearance, dressed in a dark coat and wearing a deerstalker. She thought he was over forty. Joseph Lawende saw a man with Catherine Eddowes shortly before her body was found. He said he was of middle height, dressed in a navy blue coat and wearing a deerstalker.

The amount of detail in Detective Sergeant White's statement, plus this corroborating testimony, means it was certainly White that Anderson was referring to when he wrote of 'the only person who ever had a good view of the murderer'. It was clearly White, recuperating at the Bexhill seaside home, probably from the strain and long hours he had spent on the Ripper inquiry, who identified the man Swanson called Kosminski.

We may therefore assume that Kosminski matched the description White had given of the Ripper.

But now a problem arises, because the man White identified could not have been Kosminski at all.

We know this because the real Kosminski has been traced and identified by the author Martin Fido[3], an acknowledged expert in the study of the crimes of Jack the Ripper. Fido has discovered the admissions and discharge book of the Colney Hatch asylum and also Kosminski's medical records.

The admissions book shows that Aaron Kosminski, his name misspelled as 'Kozminski', was admitted to the asylum on 7th February, 1891, suffering from 'mania'. He was discharged to Leavesden asylum in 1894, where he died in 1919. He had lived with his brother off the Commercial Road in Whitechapel and had been treated at the Mile End Old Town Workhouse in July,

3) *The Crimes, Detection and Death of Jack the Ripper*, by Martin Fido.

1890, and again in February, 1891. The records show that Kosminski was the right age, in the right place, had the right family background and the right name. There is no doubt that this is the man named by Chief Inspector Swanson.

The difficulty comes when the medical notes are examined. These reveal that he suffered from the delusion that he knew what everyone else was thinking and that he must not accept food from other people. He therefore picked up food from the gutter. He also believed he should never take a bath. The medical authorities formed the view that he was a harmless imbecile who was neither a danger to himself or anyone else.

Clearly this shambling wreck bore no resemblance to the descriptions of Jack the Ripper. Detective Sergeant White and the other witnesses had seen a tall, well dressed, cultured man. Kosminski was filthy, unable to hold an intelligent conversation and scavenged his food from the street.

The conclusion is inescapable: the man identified by White at Bexhill was an imposter using the name and background of the real Kosminski, knowing he would be unable to protest. Jack the Ripper was fortunate that White refused to testify against a fellow Jew and he was also fortunate that the division of responsibility in the investigation between the Metropolitan Police and the City of London Police allowed him to escape justice.

White was a member of the Metropolitan Police and it was this force which had arrested Jack the Ripper after the murder of Mary Jane Kelly and arranged for the identification to be made. After they were forced to release him, it was the City police who were ordered to keep Kosminski under observation. There is no reason to suppose that the City officers had any idea what the suspect looked like. They would have been given the name Aaron Kosminski and his brother's address and told to watch him. When he was eventually committed to the asylum at Colney Hatch a report would have gone to Scotland Yard. Anderson and Swanson would have believed that it was their Kosminski who had been caged; the City police would have been convinced they had been watching the right man all along.

Once Kosminski was committed, the case was closed. The result was not satisfactory, but the series of murders was over. There may have been those officers who felt the murderer should have been named, but they were over-ruled by Robert Anderson who, as he said in his book, was 'almost tempted to disclose the identity of the murderer ... but no public benefit would result from such a course'.

Meanwhile, Jack the Ripper had outwitted the police, successfully placed a scapegoat in custody and was still at large, his identity unknown.

The man who should have been able to unravel the mystery of Jack the Ripper was Sherlock Holmes, but here there is a parallel to the 'curious incident of the dog in the night time'[4]. As Holmes pointed out to Inspector Gregson, the fact that the dog did nothing was the curious incident. The fact that Sherlock Holmes apparently did nothing with regard to the Whitechapel murders is equally baffling. We know that at the time of the killings he was in London and available. From 31st August, when the first murder took place, until the last on 9th November, he had seven cases. Watson gave us details of *The Greek Interpreter*, *The Sign of Four* and *The Hound of the Baskervilles*. He also mentioned in passing the Manor House case, the French Will case, the Blackmailing case and the Famous Card Scandal. He did not record the Whitechapel murders.

None of these cases would have precluded Holmes from joining the hunt for Jack the Ripper. In fact, only *The Hound of the Baskervilles* coincided with the date of any of the murders. Holmes was consulted on Tuesday, 25th September and concluded his investigation on 20th October, but did not leave London to visit the scene of the crime in Devonshire until after 30th September when the Ripper claimed his third and fourth victims. And he was back in the capital when the last of the Ripper victims died on 9th November. In fact, Holmes's reluc-

---

4)   *The Devil's Foot*

tance to leave London in September of 1888 may be a first hint that he had a rôle in the murders; it was necessary that someone go to Devonshire at that time, but claiming his practice demanded he stay in London, Holmes sent Watson in his place.

If Holmes had been involved in some secret activity connected with the outrages in the East End and had decided not to confide in Dr Watson, it is not safe to assume that Watson would have noticed anything out of the ordinary. The doctor was not a naturally observant man. In May the previous year, Holmes had told him, "You see, but you do not observe." Watson, of course, had been preoccupied throughout 1888. His first wife, Constance Adams, had died the previous December and he had given up his medical practice in Kensington to return to Baker Street. His first attempt at authorship, *A Study in Scarlet*, had appeared in *Beeton's Christmas Annual, 1887*, and had dashed his hopes of making his fortune with his pen. It had been received with indifference by public and critic alike. Then in the September of 1888 he had fallen in love with Mary Morstan, who, in May the following year, would become his second wife. So with only a brief interlude, Dr Watson went from grief and mourning to love and courtship, suffering along the way the disappointment of the initial failure of his first book. It would be unsurprising if his undeveloped powers of observation were even less acute for the whole of 1888.

But if Watson was functioning at a level somewhat below normal at this time, then Sherlock Holmes was in a far worse condition. His addiction to cocaine was well-established and he was also in the habit of using morphine. He had failed in several important cases and he was becoming afraid that he was losing those powers that had made his fortune.

In the April of 1888 he was, in his own words, 'badly in need of a case. That is not to say that he needed money; the Baker Street coffers were comfortably full and in *The Dying Detective*, Watson remarked that the payments to Mrs Hudson had become 'princely'[5], leaving him in little doubt that the whole house could have been purchased for the price Holmes had paid for the apartment in the years that he and Watson were together. The reason he needed a successful investigation was to prove to himself that his powers of observation, deduction and reasoning were undiminished and that his drug dependency had not destroyed his abilities as a detective.

The death of John Openshaw had been a shattering blow to his self-confidence and his use of cocaine and morphine had added to his fears. He knew the dire consequences that an addiction such as his could have on the mind of the victim and the depths of degradation that those who used narcotics could sink to. Watson had warned him of the effects of cocaine abuse. "Your brain may, as you say, be aroused and excited, but it is a pathological and morbid process, which involves increased tissue change, and may at last leave a permanent weakness." Watson could have added that one of the most noticeable effects of cocaine addiction was paranoia.

Medical science now knows a great deal more about this drug than was dreamed of in the nineteenth century. One of the world authorities is Chris Ellgin-Johanson PhD of the University of Chicago Medical School, who has set out the main symptoms of dependency in *Cocaine - A New Epidemic.*

According to Dr Ellgin-Johanson, the psychoses produced by the drug so closely resemble schizophrenia that physicians often have difficulty distinguishing from drug-induced conditions and true psychiatric disorders. The user suffers delusions of persecution and paranoia, and may have chronic insomnia. We see evidence of these symptoms in Holmes throughout Watson's reports. Further effects of cocaine abuse include failing job performance, depression, anxiety and irritability. All of these are consistent with Holmes's behaviour in 1887 and 1888.

A case soon presented itself which gave Sherlock Holmes the

---

5) Flats in London varied widely in rent. Grosvenor Mansions apartments, for example, cost £425 a year in the late 1880s. Holmes and Watson were paying £200 per annum between them for full board when first they took upon residence in Baker Street.

opportunity to test himself. On Saturday, 7th April, 1888, he was consulted by Mr Grant Munro of Norbury[6] in a matter recorded by Watson under the title *The Yellow Face*. Mr Munro was concerned at the odd behaviour of his wife and, after considering the facts, Holmes deduced bigamy by Mrs Munro and blackmail by her first, in fact her only genuine, husband. He was wrong in every particular and, when the matter was concluded, spent the evening at Baker Street brooding silently over his failure.

There were equally significant failures by Sherlock Holmes in each of the next three cases recorded by Watson. All of them took place in September when the Jack the Ripper terror was at its height. *The Greek Interpreter* found Holmes delaying going to the rescue of a kidnap victim until he obtained a warrant to enter the premises where he was being held[7]. The victim died and Holmes's client came close to death. In *The Sign of Four* Holmes planned an elaborate strategy to apprehend the villains. This resulted in a spectacular chase on the Thames in steam launches, but when the criminals were caught it was discovered they had thrown overboard a vast treasure belonging to the client and it was lost forever. Inspector Athelney Jones pointed out that he would have had a body of police ready to arrest the gang before they boarded their yacht and there can be little doubt that such a plan would have resulted in the arrest of the miscreants and the recovery of the property. Finally, in *The Hound of the Baskervilles*, Holmes put his client's life at risk twice, failed to gather any significant evidence against the villain and then let him escape into a marsh and assumed, without evidence, that he had been drowned.

None of these cases was a success for Sherlock Holmes and he would still have felt the need to prove himself. His cocaine addiction was very much in evidence and in *The Sign of Four* he

6) A semi-rural suburb of London, administratively in the county of Surrey. It contained numerous isolated houses and was served by a railway station.

7) Holmes waited at Scotland Yard until Inspector Gregson could be located. The police officer would then have had to find a Justice of the Peace before he could get a warrant to enter the premises.

injected himself in front of Watson and then went on to consult with a client while still under the influence of the drug. There can be no doubt his insecurities would have made certain that he took an active interest in the events in Whitechapel. Since Watson gave us no indication of how this interest manifested itself, we must look elsewhere for the answer. It is time we examined the murders themselves.

Jack the Ripper is widely perceived as a silent, invisible fiend, a phantom who materialised, did his grisly work, and then disappeared without trace. In fact, there was a mass of evidence collected in 1888 and much of it survives today. In addition to the biographical details of the victims, the inquest transcripts and post mortem reports, there were statements from people who knew the victims, had seen them shortly before the murders or had been involved in the discovery of the bodies.

There were other clues; a mysterious piece of graffiti chalked on a wall close to where a blood-stained piece of clothing that may have belonged to Catherine Eddowes was found; a number of letters to police or news organisations purporting to come from the murderer; an envelope concealed beneath the body of Annie Chapman; and some fruit pips found near the corpse of Elizabeth Stride.

The significance of the individual elements of this body of evidence has exercised both official and amateur investigators over the years. However, some of it can be quickly disposed of: the Ripper letters, for example, were almost certainly fakes. There were dozens of these, most of which were patently the work of cranks and were immediately discarded by police. Four letters were treated more seriously by the detectives, however. The first, postmarked 28th September, 1888, used the name 'Jack the Ripper' for the first time. A second, posted 1st October, referring to the 'double event', was taken to mean the murders of Stride and Eddowes on the same night. Since reports of these killings had not appeared in the papers when the letter was posted, police considered the possibility that the writer had direct knowledge of the murders. A third letter was sent to George Lusk who was head of the Whitechapel Vigilance Committee. It was headed 'From Hell' and included a parcel containing part of a kidney. A fourth letter was sent to the pathologist who examined the kidney and was postmarked 29th October.

None of these letters was considered authentic. Robert Anderson dismissed them as 'the creation of an enterprising journalist' and Sir Melville Macnaghten claimed to have 'shrewd suspicions as to the actual author'. If the perpetrator had been a journalist it would explain how he knew about the 'double event' after it had happened, but before news appeared in the papers.

The graffiti can also be dismissed. This was found chalked on a wall in Goulston Street, about a third of a mile from Mitre Square where the body of Eddowes was found. It read: "The Juwes are not The men that Will be Blamed for nothing." It was linked to the murder because a piece of cloth stained with what may have been blood - although this has never been established - was found nearby. The cloth may have come from the apron that Eddowes was wearing when she was killed, but even that is by no means certain.

The meaning of the words has never been ascertained. Various theories have been advanced about the significance of the word 'Juwes', but none has achieved any degree of acceptance. At the time, Metropolitan Police Commissioner Sir Charles Warren believed there was an anti-semitic significance and, concerned about a possible mob reaction, ordered the message obliterated. He did not believe there was any link with the murders. If Jack the Ripper had wanted to leave a message, even one as impenetrable as this, he would have been more likely to have placed it close to the body where no one would have had any doubt about its importance or authorship. He would not have chalked it, at random, on a wall a ten minute walk away.

The most important evidence that is available is the eye-witness testimony of people who actually saw Jack the Ripper. We know from Detective Sergeant White and the others precisely what the Whitechapel murderer looked like - he looked like Sherlock Holmes, even down to the familiar deerstalker.

This characteristic headgear had been in evidence from the very beginning. Immediately after the first of the Ripper murders, that of Mary Ann Nichols, a manhunt was launched for a man known only as 'Leather Apron' from the distinctive tradesman's garment he habitually wore. This person, who was said to have attacked and threatened prostitutes in Whitechapel, was never traced, although a number of men suspected of being him were rounded up by police before being released for lack of evidence. Although his name was never discovered, 'Leather Apron' was apparently well-known by sight and several people familiar with him said he was later seen at a lodging house in Dorset Street, the scene of the last of the Ripper murders. All of the witnesses said he wore a deerstalker hat.

The physical similarities between Sherlock Holmes and Jack the Ripper are quite striking. Detective Sergeant White, who gave the most complete description, put the suspect's age at thirty-three; in 1888, Holmes would have been thirty-four. White said the Ripper's face was long and thin; Watson wrote that Holmes had a narrow face. White remarked on the suspect's 'extraordinarily brilliant' eyes; Watson recorded that Holmes had 'sharp and piercing eyes'. According to White, the man he saw emerging from the alley had jet black hair; Watson told us that Holmes's hair was black. White particularly noticed the suspect's hands which were 'snow white' with 'long and tapering' fingers. Watson said us that Holmes had 'long, white hands'.

The only discrepancy appears to be the issue of height. White put the suspect at about five feet ten inches. Watson said Holmes was 'rather over six feet', but there is some evidence in *The Three Students* that Watson had overstated his friend's stature.

A resemblance to the suspect, albeit a strong one, does not of course constitute a case for prosecution. Neither does the fact that Holmes did not have an alibi for the times of any of the murders. There are other qualities which he shared with Jack the Ripper.

The inquest transcripts and post mortem reports make it clear that the killer would have needed some basic skill in anatomy to carry out the crude dissection of the corpses; it may be fairly deduced that he would have needed a comprehensive knowledge of the geography of the East End in order to move swiftly from place to place without attracting attention; he would have required a base in Whitechapel so that he could get off the streets quickly and change bloodstained clothing; and he would have needed the physical ability to overcome his victims.

Sherlock Holmes possessed all of these. Dr Watson recorded that the detective had an accurate, if unsystematic, knowledge of anatomy[8]; he frequently operated in the East End, spending several days there on at least one occasion; he had several 'small refuges' in different parts of London[9] and it is not unreasonable to assume one of these was in the vicinity of Whitechapel; and physically, we know from Watson, that Holmes was a skilled boxer[10], had an expert knowledge of the Japanese wrestling technique known as Baritsu[11], was 'always in training'[12] and had 'a grasp of iron'[13]. He would have had no difficulty in subduing any of the murder victims.

The weight of circumstantial evidence against Holmes is quite overwhelming: he matched the description of the Ripper; he had no alibi; he had a basic knowledge of anatomy; he had an expert knowledge of the East End and probably had a hideout there. But to clinch the case some kind of physical evidence is needed, a clue which will lead directly to Sherlock Holmes.

In fact there are two. First, some fruit pips, probably from grapes, which were found close to the body of Elizabeth Stride, and, second, an envelope that was discovered beneath the body of Annie Chapman.

Elizabeth Stride's body was found at about 1.00 a.m. in Dutfield's Yard in Berner Street. Constable Walter Dew, who

8) *A Study in Scarlet.*
9) *Black Peter.*
10) *The Five Orange Pips*; *A Study in Scarlet.*
11) *The Empty House.*
12) *The Solitary Cyclist.*
13) *His Last Bow.*

was one of the officers called to the scene, later recalled that a number of grape stones were found on the ground close to the body. The following day the London *Evening News* published a report quoting Matthew Packer who owned a shop at 44 Berner Street, two doors away from Dutfield's Yard. He told the reporter that a man, accompanied by Stride, had bought some grapes from him shortly before the body was discovered. We know that Stride did not eat any of the grapes. The post mortem examination report lists the contents of her stomach. It contained cheese, potatoes and some farinaceous powder, but there was no trace of fruit. It is apparent, therefore, that they had been eaten by her companion and the pips placed on the ground by him. They had been left so that they were obvious to the most casual observer ... even a Scotland Yard man. But how did they get there? The Ripper was a fast worker; he certainly would not have stood around eating grapes before getting on with the business to hand. He must have eaten the fruit while walking with Stride from the shop to the yard. Instead of spitting out the pips or throwing them away, he had retained them for future use.

His purpose was to leave a warning. The pips warned of death and the Ripper fully intended to commit two murders that night. He was leaving a message that Stride was simply the first victim of his planned 'double event'. Sherlock Holmes was fully aware of the significance of such a warning. In *The Five Orange Pips*, that case which had dealt such a shattering blow to his self-confidence, the pips had been sent to John Openshaw shortly before he was murdered. Now Jack the Ripper was leaving a similar warning beside his victim.

The fact that the warning comprised grape stones rather than orange pips is of no importance. Holmes knew that the type of fruit had no bearing on the significance of the message. "Melon seeds or orange pips", he told Watson in the Openshaw case, each carried the same threat. And he sent a similar warning to the man he believed responsible for Openshaw's death. Watson watched in surprise as: "He took an orange from the cupboard, and tearing it to pieces, he squeezed out the pips upon the table. Of these he took five, and thrust them into an envelope."

Who, other than Sherlock Holmes, could have placed such a taunting and evocative clue at the scene of the murder of Elizabeth Stride?

The envelope found beneath the body of Annie Chapman can also be linked to Holmes. This was postmarked: 'London, 28 Aug., 1888'. On the back it bore the seal of the Sussex Regiment; on the front was inscribed the letter 'M'. The Sussex connection is of prime importance. The Openshaw family, in the case which had troubled Holmes so greatly, lived on an estate in Sussex, just south of the town of Horsham and John Openshaw was recommended to Holmes by a Major Prendergast who Holmes had helped in an earlier matter. There is therefore a chain of evidence linking Holmes with Sussex and the army.

As to the inscription on the front of the envelope, this strongly echoes the reference two years later in *The Final Problem* to the pigeonhole marked 'M' wherein Holmes kept the evidence relating to the Moriarty gang. Can there be any doubt that it referred to the Professor?

A hypothesis can now be constructed. Sherlock Holmes, in the guise of Kosminski, the unfortunate imbecile whose identity he assumed, is the author of the five murders attributed to Jack the Ripper. He was seen with the victims on three occasions and his description was widely circulated. He used his expert knowledge of the East End and the hideout he kept there to evade capture. His physical strength and knowledge of Baritsu enabled him to easily subdue his victims and his accurate, if unsystematic, knowledge of anatomy enabled him to carry out the mutilation which he regarded as necessary. He had no alibi for any of the murders and he specifically avoided leaving London in the Baskerville case so that he could commit the 'double event'.

In his cocaine-driven paranoia he still needed to prove himself the greatest of all detectives and, to this end, he left what he regarded as an obvious clue - the grape pips - near the body of his third victim.

He was unaware that he had already left a clue - the envelope - at the scene of the second murder. Finally he was arrested by the Metropolitan Police under the alias Kosminski. He was not recognised as Sherlock Holmes, because it would be some eight years before he achieved fame through the medium of Dr Watson's stories in *The Strand* magazine.

Then he was dealt an extraordinary piece of good fortune. He was taken to Bexhill on Sea where Detective Sergeant White was at the seaside convalescent home recovering from overwork and exhaustion brought on by his efforts in the Ripper case. White immediately identified him as Jack the Ripper, but, believing him to be Kosminski, a fellow Jew, he refused to testify against him. Holmes was therefore taken back to Whitechapel and, since the police have no evidence against him, released.

The Metropolitan Police, who made the arrest, did not intend, however, to let matters rest there. The suspect was to be kept under surveillance in the hope that he would betray himself. But the job of watching him was given to an entirely different police force, the City of London Police. They were simply given a name, Aaron Kosminski, and an address and told that he was suspected of being Jack the Ripper and must not be let out of their sight. The City force swung into action and mounted an operation to keep the suspect under observation. But neither police force was aware that the man identified as the Ripper and the man being watched were two separate individuals. Eventually the real Kosminski was committed to an asylum, but Jack the Ripper remained at liberty.

It is worth noting at this stage that there is one hint in Dr Watson's writings that Sherlock Holmes may have been in Bexhill at the time Detective Sergeant White was identifying Jack the Ripper. In his account of the case of *The Greek Interpreter*, Watson referred to the 'Manor House case'. There is a well-known manor house in Bexhill close to the site of the police 'seaside home'. It is now the town museum, but this may have provided Holmes with an explanation to Watson for his enforced journey to the coast.

Two questions remain. What drove Holmes to commit these terrible crimes? And, what forced him to stop?

Serial sex killers like Jack the Ripper are notoriously difficult to catch because, unlike other murderers, they strike at random; there is no motive in the accepted sense, rather there is a compulsion. This has been defined by scientists and there is now a psychological profile of the typical serial killer which is available to law enforcement agencies.

In his history of forensic detection[14], Colin Wilson, sets it out: "... the serial killer is a recognisable type in case after case, the same patterns repeat themselves with almost monotonous regularity: deprivation of affection in childhood, sadism towards animals, fear and distrust of women, alcohol and drug abuse, resentment towards society, high dominance and the tendency to escape into a world of fantasy."

Even those with only a passing knowledge of Holmes's character will realise that he exhibited each of these traits. There is, for example, clear evidence [see Chapter Two] that he was starved of affection, particularly by his father, when he was a child. On occasion he acted in a sadistic manner, beating the subjects in the dissecting room at Bart's Hospital with a stick, carrying out grotesque experiments in seeing how far a harpoon would penetrate a pig's carcass and torturing the unfortunate Percy Phelps with the discovery of the naval treaty.

His distrust of women is well-known. "I am not a whole-souled admirer of womankind," he remarked in *The Valley of Fear* and in *The Sign of Four*, he observed, "Women are never to be entirely trusted - not the best of them." His addiction to cocaine and morphine was well documented by Dr Watson as was his rejection of society. Watson said he "loathed every form of society with his whole Bohemian soul".

There is no doubt that Holmes was a natural leader and he fitted into that five per cent of the population who can be classed

14) *Written in Blood*, London, 1989.

as 'highly dominant'. This group is defined as unusually talented and dominant men who actually achieve eminence. Lastly, there is ample evidence of Holmes's tendency to escape into fantasy, inflating the number and importance of his cases and withdrawing into himself with the aid of music. In short, Sherlock Holmes exhibits all of the classic psychological symptoms that identify the serial killer.

Not all men who match this profile go on to commit sex murders. It is a fact of forensic science that a series of killings, such as those carried out by Jack the Ripper, are often triggered by a single traumatic event. If we examine the events of 1888 we can identify an occurrence which would have been so shattering for Sherlock Holmes that it could have released Jack the Ripper.

On 7th August a prostitute called Martha Tabram was murdered in the East End by a soldier she had picked up in the Angel and Crown pub near Whitechapel Church. She received thirty-nine stab wounds which were thought to have been inflicted with a bayonet. The attack was so savage that in months to come, detectives would investigate to see if there were enough similarities with the later murders to consider it a Ripper killing, a theory that was quickly discarded. This occurred at a time when Holmes, in his cocaine-induced paranoia, felt a desperate need to prove himself. He was plagued by self-doubt and failure.

The reason that the murder of this drab, middle-aged woman should have had such an effect on him was that he thought he knew her. Mrs Tabram also went by the name Martha Turner and Holmes would have assumed that she was the self-same Mrs Turner who had appeared briefly in the Irene Adler affair[15] posing as the housekeeper. Martha Turner had been a minor member of Holmes's organisation and if she was now brutally murdered, it was stark evidence that he could not even protect his own helpers. Perhaps he reasoned that the cause of her death had been prostitution and that to rid the East End of whores would prevent such an event happening again. Whatever the processes of his tortured mind, this murder could have been the event

15) *A Scandal in Bohemia.*

which unleashed Jack the Ripper.

The murders ceased with the killing of Mary Jane Kelly on 9th November. Forensic scientists have learned that serial killers do not voluntarily cease their activities. They stop only when they are arrested or, in some other way, are physically prevented from continuing their atrocities. Something must have prevented Holmes from seeking out more victims.

Mary Jane Kelly, the last of the Ripper's victims, was also the youngest. There is evidence to suggest that before going to the East End she had worked in central London as a domestic servant, being placed by the Bellord Domestic Agency. She may well have been the maid, Mary Jane, who was dismissed by Dr Watson's wife because she was incorrigibly clumsy and careless in May, 1887[16]. Without a reference she would have been unable to find another position and it is far from unlikely that a year and a half later would have descended to earning a living as a common prostitute in Whitechapel.

The horror as Holmes realised he had murdered the former servant girl of his friend and partner may have precipitated some form of psychiatric reaction that even Watson would have noticed. If so, he would have been obliged, as Holmes's medical adviser, to take action. We cannot know for sure what the crisis was, but we know from Dr Watson that Holmes took on no further work from mid-October, 1888, when the Baskerville case was concluded, until the following April, when he and Watson were involved in the case of *The Copper Beeches*.

This six-month hiatus stands out at a time when Holmes was becoming increasingly busy with an ever-increasing workload. To discover what he was doing in this period, it is necessary to look at the case of *The Missing Threequarter* which took place eight years later in 1896. Here Watson reports on his successful efforts to wean Holmes from his drug addiction. Throughout 1888 there were indications from the doctor's frequent remarks and warnings

16) *Ibid.*

that he was becoming concerned about his friend's addiction. After that year there was no mention of drug dependency until Watson's later comment. The conclusion is clear: Watson was prompted by Holmes's mental condition in or about November of 1888 to resolve the narcotics problem once and for all.

He would have taken what were the standard steps in Victorian England to cure such an addiction. This would have involved forcibly confining the patient until his craving for the drug ceased. Thus, Jack the Ripper would have been physically prevented from continuing his series of murders. When Holmes was released, his addiction was under control, his paranoia had receded and the urge to kill had disappeared. There is some confirmation of this in *The Copper Beeches*. In this report, Holmes is shown to be ill-tempered and testy, classic features of long-term narcotic withdrawal.

After a few months confinement, Sherlock Holmes was free once more to resume his career. He could again manipulate the rich and influential, preying on them when they were at their most vulnerable, just as he preyed on the weak and unprotected women of the East End. He could continue to abuse the society he loathed, just as he abused his own body with drugs and alcohol. The murders had been one outward sign of his contempt for his fellow human beings; his life of blackmail, fraud and corruption was yet another.

Like the police and the public, Dr Watson never learned the terrible truth about Jack the Ripper. It was a secret destined to remain buried deep in the tortured soul of Sherlock Holmes.

CHAPTER EIGHT

The Exceptional Policeman

The Wisteria Lodge affair in the spring of 1890 was a successful and well-handled investigation following a string of indifferent cases for Sherlock Holmes. It was unfortunate that it was a member of that much-despised body, the official police force, who brought the matter to a conclusion. Holmes was left standing by Inspector Baynes of the Surrey Constabulary.

The investigation, which led to the Tiger of San Pedro, followed a string of cases in which Holmes acted in an eccentric, dangerous or ineffectual manner.

After the terrible events of 1888, he took up his practice once more in April of the following year with the case of *The Copper Beeches*, which, despite his ill-tempered manner, he managed to settle quite satisfactorily. It was a different matter in *The Boscombe Valley Mystery* in which Holmes allowed a killer to go free and subjected an innocent man to a capital trial. The facts are these: a blackmailer had been killed by his victim and the blackmailer's son had been arrested and charged with the crime. Holmes, however, was content for the innocent man to be put through the ordeal of a trial in which a guilty verdict would have meant the death penalty. The reason for this strange conduct was that the real killer, the blackmail victim, had a terminal disease and was soon to die. Holmes took the precaution of obtaining from the killer a confession which, he warned, he would use if the innocent man was wrongly condemned.

It is a highly questionable action under any circumstances and it is fortunate for the wrongly-accused man that all went as Holmes planned. A guilty verdict and a death sentence might have been difficult things to reverse, even for Sherlock Holmes. His one witness was slowly dying and the confession, if it had been produced posthumously, may have carried less weight in the Appeal Court than Holmes expected. His explanation as to why he waited for the jury to reach a verdict before producing it would have also appeared a little thin. And, there again, what would have happened if some misadventure had befallen Holmes? It was an unwarranted risk and one that could have resulted in the death of an innocent man on the gallows.

On 15th June, 1889, Sherlock Holmes called on Watson in Paddington where he had set up in practice following his marriage to Mary Morstan[1]. Holmes wanted the doctor to go with him to Birmingham to help in the case of *The Stockbroker's Clerk*.

The case concerned an attempt to rob a City of London financial house. A clerk, Hall Pycroft, had been lured away by the robbers and was being impersonated by one of them. Holmes managed to work out what had happened as far as the clerk was concerned, but read in a newspaper that the robbers had been arrested by two policemen after leaving the building with their loot. During the robbery they had murdered a nightwatchman. A man was dead and the case can hardly be regarded as a triumph for Sherlock Holmes.

Holmes behaved rather oddly in *The Naval Treaty* in July, 1889. He had successfully unravelled the problem of the missing treaty which had threatened the Foreign Office career of Watson's old school friend, Percy 'Tadpole' Phelps, and identified the guilty men, but when he came to reveal the result of his inquiry, his action was extremely odd. Phelps had been severely ill with 'brain fever' yet Holmes chose to make him lift the cover of a dish under which he had hidden the recovered treaty. For Holmes this might have been an amusing practical joke, but the effect on Phelps was somewhat dramatic. He stared at the treaty, his face as white as a sheet, and then snatched up the document and

1)   Miss Morstan became Mrs John H. Watson on 1st May, 1889, when they were married at St Mark's in Camberwell. The first Mrs Watson had died in December, 1887. (*Sherlock Holmes, A Biography*. W.S. Baring Gould, London, 1963)

cavorted around the room shrieking before collapsing into a chair where he was revived with brandy. "I can never resist a touch of the dramatic," Holmes remarked.

The case of *The Cardboard Box* on 31st August, 1889, was a grotesque, but simple matter which was handled satisfactorily. On 8th September, Watson brought Victor Hatherley to Baker Street and there commenced *The Adventure of the Engineer's Thumb*. In this the crime had already been committed, the villains had made good their escape and there was little for Sherlock Holmes to do. Indeed, his presence did not have any effect on the way things turned out. *The Crooked Man* affair on 11th September was proved by medical evidence to be no crime at all and although Holmes located an important witness, there was again little he could do to influence events.

None of these cases would have done anything to restore Holmes's belief in himself, but the Wisteria Lodge affair would shatter his self-esteem.

It was brought to Holmes's attention by John Scott-Eccles who, according to Watson, was 'a good citizen, orthodox and conventional to the last degree'. He had arrived in Baker Street on 24th March, 1890, in a state of some disarray, after what he described as a 'most singular and unpleasant experience'. Hard on his heels were Inspector Gregson of Scotland Yard and Inspector Baynes of the Surrey force. They had traced Scott-Eccles through the telegram[2] he had sent to warn Holmes he was coming.

Holmes was able to persuade the officers to wait while Mr Scott-Eccles told his story. The previous evening, he said, he had gone to Wisteria Lodge, between Esher and Oxshott in Surrey, to spend a few days with a new acquaintance, a young man of Spanish descent connected with the Embassy. It was a strange evening. Apart from the servants, the two of them were alone in the house and, over dinner, although the young Spaniard, Garcia,

---

2) Scott-Eccles had sent the telegram from Charing Cross Post Office, which is open twenty-four hours a day.

at first made some attempt to be entertaining, he was obviously preoccupied. Later a note arrived and then Garcia 'gave up all pretence at conversation and sat smoking endless cigarettes'.

Scott-Eccles was already regretting he had accepted the invitation and wishing he could invent some excuse to go back home. He was, therefore, glad to go to bed at about eleven. Some time later Garcia opened the door to his room and asked if he had rung, He had not. Garcia apologised for disturbing him, saying it was 'nearly one o'clock'. Scott-Eccles then dropped off to sleep, not waking until nearly nine in the morning. To his amazement the house was deserted. His host and the servants had all disappeared.

At first Scott-Eccles thought the whole thing had been an absurd joke. He checked with the land agents in the village and discovered that the rent had been paid in advance, the Spanish Embassy did not know Garcia and Scott-Eccles's friend who had introduced Garcia 'knew rather less about him than I did'. At that point, Scott-Eccles called in Sherlock Holmes.

The two police officers were able to report that Garcia had been found dead that morning on Oxshott Common, his head 'smashed to pulp by heavy blows of a sandbag or some such instrument'. There had been no attempt at robbery, but 'his assailant had gone on beating him long after he was dead'. Inspector Baynes had found the mysterious note which was delivered the previous evening where it had fallen in the back of the fire grate. In tones remarkably reminiscent of Sherlock Holmes at his best, he reported: "The note is written upon ordinary cream-laid paper without watermark. It is a quarter-sheet. The paper is cut off in two snips with a short-bladed scissors. It has been folded over three times and sealed with purple wax, put on hurriedly and pressed down with some flat, oval object. It is addressed to Mr. Garcia, Wisteria Lodge. It says: 'Our own colours, green and white. Green open, white shut. Main stair, first corridor, seventh right, green baize. God-speed. D.' It is a woman's writing, done with a sharp-pointed pen, but the address is either done with another pen or by someone else. It is thicker and bolder, as you see."

Holmes, who had already 'smiled his appreciation' at the close examination Baynes gave the house, then complimented Baynes on his attention to the detail in his examination of the note. He was, in fact, rather patronising. After telling Baynes what a splendid job he had done, Holmes remarked: "A few trifling points might perhaps be added." But he was able to supply only two and these of minor significance. The oval seal, he identified as a plain sleeve link and the scissors were bent nail scissors.

Baynes revealed that a letter found in the dead man's pocket was from Scott-Eccles accepting the invitation to stay at Wisteria Lodge, He wired Gregson to locate Scott-Eccles in London while the house was examined. Baynes, as Sherlock Holmes was quick to say, had been 'very prompt and businesslike' in his handling of the case that far. He had also established because of the rain that Garcia had been lying on the Common since one o'clock. Scott-Eccles pointed out that Garcia, whose voice was 'unmistakable', had addressed him in his room at that very hour, but Holmes dismissed the objection: "Remarkable, but by no means impossible."

Sherlock Holmes's hypothesis which he revealed to Watson after Scott-Eccles had left with the police officers was that the reason the orthodox and conventional Scott-Eccles was invited to the house was to provide an alibi. "It is likely that when Garcia went out of his way to tell [Scott-Eccles] that it was one, it was really not more than twelve". As Holmes pointed out: "If Garcia could do whatever he had to do and be back by the hour mentioned, he had evidently a powerful reply to any accusation".

As to the mysterious message. "This is an assignation. We may find a jealous husband at the bottom of it all." Holmes also collected a list of large houses in the vicinity of Wisteria Lodge and their occupants. If 'one has to ascend a main stair and seek the seventh door in a corridor, it is perfectly clear the house is a very large one'. And he added: "It is equally certain that this house cannot be more than a mile or two from Oxshott, since Garcia was walking in that direction, and hoped ... to be back in Wisteria Lodge in time to avail himself of an alibi, which could only be available up to one o'clock."

Holmes and Watson then joined Inspector Baynes in Esher to carry out an on-the-spot investigation. After an examination of the house, Holmes and Baynes agreed to work independently on the case. As Baynes said: "I should be glad to say afterwards that I had solved it without your help."

Holmes 'laughed good-humouredly' at this, greeting Baynes's remark with: "Well, well, inspector." It may have been that he was lost for words. After all, here was a police officer who could not be dismissed as a dim-witted oaf. He had kept up with Holmes so far and showed every sign of continuing to do so. Holmes may well have felt a touch of concern. If he blundered in this matter, there was a policeman who would see through any excuses, and a policeman who might well beat Sherlock Holmes to the solution. But in any event, Holmes had to make the best of things and told Baynes: "My results are always very much at your service if you care to apply to me for them."

Watson 'could tell by numerous subtle signs, which might have been lost upon anyone but myself, that Holmes was on a hot scent'. There was a 'subdued eagerness and suggestion of tension in his brightened eyes and brisker manner' which assured Watson that the game was afoot.

But exactly what it was that was afoot was a mystery to the good doctor, for Holmes after his habit said nothing and Watson in his turn did not ask. Watson, in fact, waited patiently for some sign from Holmes that things were nearing completion. But to Watson's ever-deepening disappointment he waited in vain[3].

"Day succeeded day, and my friend took no step forward ...

---

3) Holmes and Watson stayed at an inn in the village of Esher during the investigation. Watson referred to it as 'The Bull', but his memory was apparently faulty since the village inn is 'The Bear'.

he spent his days in lone, and often solitary walks, or in chatting with a number of village gossips whose acquaintance he had cultivated."

Then five days after the crime a newspaper report shocked both Holmes and Watson: "THE OXSHOTT MYSTERY ... ARREST OF SUPPOSED ASSASSIN". The report said that Baynes had arrested Garcia's former cook 'a huge and hideous mulatto' who disappeared after the crime.

Holmes dashed off to warn Baynes that he was on the wrong track, but the policeman merely thanked him for his warning and reminded him they had agreed each would work in his own way.

"There's something in Inspector Baynes which I can't quite understand," remarked Holmes.

He decided then to put Watson 'in touch with the situation' because he thought he might need the doctor's help that night.

He said that Garcia and his servants were all confederates in an unknown crime, hence the servants disappeared after Garcia was killed; Scott-Eccles was invited to Wisteria Lodge to provide an alibi and the note indicated a confederate at the other end. In the five days since the crime, Holmes had had his attention drawn to the old Jacobean grange of High Gable, less than half a mile from the scene of the tragedy. The occupant, Mr. Henderson, was, said Holmes, a curious man. Holmes claimed he had met Henderson on a pretext, but his powers of deduction seem to have failed him on that occasion. "He is either a foreigner or has lived in the Tropics," he told Watson. It is perhaps rather odd that Sherlock Holmes was unable to distinguish between a foreigner and an Englishman. But he was more positive about Henderson's friend and secretary, Mr. Lucas, who was 'undoubtedly a foreigner'. This is perhaps not too difficult to ascertain since Holmes said that Lucas was 'chocolate brown, wily, suave and cat-like with a poisonous gentleness of speech'.

In addition to the two men there was also an English governess, Miss Burnet, who looked after Henderson's two children, and a confidential man-servant as well as 'butlers, footmen, maid servants and the usual over-fed under-worked staff of a large English country house'.

Holmes had gained his information from Warner, a gardener discharged by Henderson. Things, he had discovered, were a bit odd in the Henderson household. The servants all lived in one wing; Henderson, Lucas, the man-servant, Miss Burnet and the children in the other. There was no link between the two wings other than Henderson's own servant, who served the meals. Everything was carried through one door which formed the connection. But more than this: Henderson never went out alone. Lucas was always with him, and Miss Burnet and the children hardly went out at all, except in the garden.

Holmes assumed - although there is no evidence for it - that the mysterious note received by Garcia came from the Henderson house. Who wrote it? It was a woman's writing: "Who then, but Miss Burnet?" Holmes had also discovered that Miss Burnet had not been seen since the night of Garcia's murder. "You, will appreciate the difficulty of the situation, Watson," said he. "There is nothing upon which we can apply for a warrant. The woman's disappearance counts for nothing since in that extraordinary household any member of it may be invisible for a week. And yet she may at the present moment be in danger of her life."

Holmes' action thus far had been to watch the house and leave his 'agent', the discharged gardener, to guard the gates.

Sherlock Holmes had decided the situation could not continue. "If the law can do nothing we must take the risk ourselves," he said, perhaps remembering the tragic cost of delay in *The Greek Interpreter*.

Watson did not find the prospect very attractive, but agreed to go along with Holmes's plan to break into the house that night, He was, however, saved the trouble. The gardener, Warner, arrived at Holmes's lodgings in Esher at about five o'clock. "They've gone, Mr. Holmes. They went by the last train. The lady broke away, and I've got her in a cab downstairs."

Holmes, delighted at the turn of events, sent for Baynes to

hear the woman's story. The policeman came in wreathed in smiles. "Why sir, you've got me the very evidence I want," he said. And he revealed that he had been after Henderson from the very first. He arrested the cook simply to lull Henderson into a false sense of security. Baynes also told Holmes that he had a plainclothes man at the station who would keep track of Henderson and Lucas. This was something that Sherlock Holmes had patently forgotten. While he had been waiting to question Miss Burnet, the probable murderers of Garcia had been getting further away. He had taken no action to keep track of them.

Baynes was also able to reveal who Henderson really was. Sherlock Holmes was still in the dark about the real identities of all the people involved or what the 'unknown crime' was that led Garcia to his death. In fact, all Holmes had done was identify the Henderson household as being somehow involved in the murder and guessed that Miss Burnet wrote the note to Garcia. He did not know why or what it was all about, although he had eliminated one possibility: "Miss Burnet's age and character make it certain that my first idea that there might be a love interest in our story is out of the question."

But after five days that is hardly real progress.

Baynes, however, in the same five days had identified the household as being involved in the murder, had been keeping it under observation and had been keeping the local railway station under surveillance. He had also discovered the real identity of Henderson - a crucial factor in getting to the bottom of the crime.

"Henderson," Baynes told Holmes, "is Don Murillo, once called the Tiger of San Pedro."

The name is enough for Watson: "The whole history of the man came back to me in a flash. He had made his name as the most lewd and bloodthirsty tyrant that had ever governed any country with a pretence to civilisation." His name had been a terror throughout the dozen years he was in power, Watson recalled but finally he was overthrown in a popular uprising and escaped with his children, his secretary and his wealth.

But how did Baynes uncover this when Holmes did not? "If you look it up," he told Holmes, "you will find that the San Pedro colours are green and white, same as in the note."

It was there all the time, but Holmes failed to spot it. Baynes meanwhile had traced Henderson back through 'Paris and Rome and Madrid to Barcelona, where his ship came in in '86.' And he has the motive: "They've been looking for him all the time for their revenge, but it is only now that they have begun to find him out."

The only question still to be answered was asked by Holmes: "How came you into this matter, Miss Burnet? How can an English lady join in such a murderous affair?"

"...because there is no other way in the world by which justice can be gained," she replied.

Miss Burnet - who was not really a 'miss' at all - explained that her husband was shot in San Pedro on Murillo's order. She and some others had been seeking revenge on him ever since. She joined his staff as governess to his children to be in a better position to keep track of the former dictator. On the night Garcia was killed, he was to have assassinated Murillo. Miss Burnet had to write final instructions to him - the note - but somehow she 'excited the suspicion' of the secretary, Lucas, and he discovered her just as she finished the note.

The ex-dictator and his secretary decided that to murder Miss Burnet was too dangerous, but determined to get rid of Garcia. They sent the note and it lured him to his death.

It was to be some time before Murillo finally faced justice. He managed to evade his police shadow in London and disappeared for some six months. He and Lucas were eventually killed in a Madrid hotel room.

For Sherlock Holmes it was something of a disturbing case, one in which he made little progress while his rival, the police inspector, managed to have everything sewn up at every turn. Even Holmes's aid to Miss Burnet was a matter of luck, luck that she tried to escape while Holmes's man was on the spot and lucky the former gardener was able to get her away.

Sherlock Holmes dealt with six more cases in 1890. Watson mentioned, but did not detail, the case of Morgan, the poisoner, the affair of Merridew 'of abominable memory', the case of Mathews and the service Holmes performed for the royal family of Scandinavia. The doctor has, however, left us with the complete records of *Silver Blaze* and *The Beryl Coronet*.

Silver Blaze showed Holmes, erratic as ever, at his brilliant best, successfully solving a horse-racing mystery. How, after a catalogue of failure, he should be able to come back in such a way, is an almost insoluble mystery in itself. However, in the early stages of the case Holmes admitted to a blunder. The affair surrounded the disappearance of the racehorse Silver Blaze and the death of the trainer, John Straker. Holmes received telegrams from both the owner of the horse and the local police inspector on Tuesday, 23rd September, but did not decide to go to Dartmoor, where the tragedy occurred, until Thursday, 25th September.

Holmes's blunder, which he wryly remarked to Watson was 'a more common occurrence than anyone would think who only knew me through your memoirs', was that he 'could not believe it possible that the most remarkable horse in England could long remain concealed, especially in so sparsely inhabited a place as Dartmoor'. Holmes had expected to hear at any time that the horse had been found and that his abductor was the murderer of John Straker.

In *The Beryl Coronet* there is a different Sherlock Holmes entirely. He unscrambled a somewhat simple mystery, placing the blame where it belonged. But he is seen to demand a fee in relation not to the amount of work that he had put in, but to the scandal which has been averted. He claimed to have paid three thousand pounds to a receiver to recover three missing gemstones. When his client got his chequebook out, Holmes, thinking of his fee, told him: "Better make it out for four thousand pounds."

There is considerable doubt as to whether Holmes actually paid out the three thousand in the first place. The question is not whether a fee of one thousand pounds is justified, rather it is a question of whether Holmes swindled his client out of an additional three thousand for his night's work.

Although a successful exploit, *The Beryl Coronet* showed yet again the unsavoury side of Sherlock Holmes's character. More than that, it demonstrated how his career lurched from poverty to vast success, to incompetence and breakdown, to unscrupulous and illegal behaviour.

But Holmes was not yet at the lowest point of his career - albeit that he was showing outward signs of success - and he was on the point of making his greatest error.

Dr John Watson on holiday in Scotland in 1893.

CHAPTER NINE

A Murder in Cold Blood

Sherlock Holmes's campaign against Professor Moriarty reached its peak in April, 1891. It was on the evening of Friday, 24th April, that Holmes walked into Watson's consulting room[1] 'looking even paler and thinner than usual'.

"I have been a little pressed of late," said Holmes. "Have you any objection to my closing your shutters?"

"You are afraid of something?" Watson asked.

"Well I am," came the reply.

"Of what?"

"Of airguns."

Watson was puzzled by the conversation, especially when Holmes announced his intention of leaving the house by clambering over the back garden wall. Watson, it must be remembered, was not living in Baker Street at that time. He had married and, as he points out in *The Final Problem*, had not been closely in touch with Holmes. In fact, he says it was only from the newspapers that he knew the whereabouts of Sherlock Holmes in the winter of 1890 and the spring of 1891. He had, of course, forgotten his visit to Baker Street in December, possibly to take a gift or invite Holmes for Christmas dinner, when he witnessed the events of *The Beryl Coronet*. But, that aside, Watson had clearly had no contact with Holmes since the previous September when they were involved in the case of *Silver Blaze*.

So Watson had no way of knowing what had been happening, but he had seen the way things had been going for Holmes over

---

1) This refers to Dr Watson's practice in Paddington. He had bought it from old Mr Farquhar prior to his marriage to Mary Morstan in May, 1889 (*The Stockbroker's Clerk*) and it had increased steadily (*The Engineer's Thumb*).

the past few years. The shock and guilt over the death of John Openshaw, the drug addiction, the constant failures that played on Holmes's mind: all had been worrying for Watson as Holmes's medical adviser. However, after the Silver Blaze case Watson, no doubt, hoped his friend was over the worst of the problems afflicting him. But when Holmes suggested they should spend a week away on the Continent, Watson knew something was seriously wrong. "There was something very strange in all this," he says in *The Final Problem*. And indeed there was. Something about Holmes's pale, worn face told Watson that his nerves were at their highest tension. And it is clear that he realised Holmes's grip on reality, which had been slipping since he worked himself to a collapse while looking into the affairs of the Netherland-Sumatra Company in 1887, had not finally gone.

Holmes's next question no doubt further shocked Watson. "You have probably never heard of Professor Moriarty?" he asked.

Of course Watson had heard of Professor Moriarty. It was only a little over three years earlier, at the time of *The Valley of Fear*, that Holmes had said to him: "You have heard me speak of Professor Moriarty?"

Watson at that time had been familiar enough with the subject to make a joke of his answer: "The famous scientific criminal, as famous among crooks as -"

"My blushes, Watson," Holmes had murmured, falling into Watson's trap.

"I was about to say 'as he is unknown to the public'," the doctor had successfully concluded.

Watson had not forgotten the Professor in the space of three years and Holmes surely could not have forgotten that Watson had been with him throughout the events of *The Valley of Fear*. The question was so out of character, and so obviously demanded a negative answer, that Watson decided to play along with Holmes, to humour him. "Never," he replied firmly.

This was the reaction that Holmes wanted. It enabled him to

launch into a verbal attack on Moriarty. "The man pervades London, and no-one has heard of him," he told Watson. "That's what puts him on a pinnacle in the records of crime." Holmes said that if he could free society of Moriarty he would feel his own career 'had reached its summit'.

Watson was still perplexed. He had heard Holmes's allegations about Moriarty before. But Watson, like the CID, felt that Holmes had 'a bee in his bonnet' over the Professor. And by Holmes's own admission he had not one shred of evidence against Moriarty to link him with any crime.

"What has he done, then?" asked Watson.

For reply Holmes listed Moriarty's life and achievements: of good birth; endowed with a phenomenal mathematical faculty; at twenty-one wrote a treatise on the binomial theorem which had a European vogue; won the mathematical chair at 'one of our smaller universities'; was compelled to resign after 'dark rumours' surrounded him in the university town; went to London and set up as an army coach. He could have also mentioned that Moriarty was also the celebrated author of *The Dynamics of an Asteroid*, a work that may have foreshadowed Einstein's theory of relativity.

That much was known to the world, but Holmes claimed he had discovered much more. For a long time he had been aware of the existence of a 'deep organizing power which for ever stands in the way of the law and throws its shield over the wrong doer'. What he meant, of course, was that when Sherlock Holmes failed then it had to be something pretty formidable that he was up against. In Holmes's twisted view of things it was entirely logical: Sherlock Holmes was the world's greatest detective, if he failed then his opponent must be his equal; an opponent who was his equal had to be a master criminal and if he was a master criminal then he was probably involved in most of the crime in England, and Europe as well come to that.

Holmes had no new evidence to offer about the arch-criminal. He claimed: "For years I have endeavoured to break through the veil which shrouded it, and at last the time came when I seized my thread and followed it until it led me after a thousand cunning windings, to ex-Professor Moriarty of mathematical celebrity."

Here is firm evidence that Holmes is suffering some mental breakdown. He has now come to believe that he, Sherlock Holmes, suspected the existence of the criminal mastermind and traced the thread to Moriarty. He has entirely forgotten the intervention of 'Fred Porlock', Holmes's somewhat unreliable informer on the subject of the Professor. Holmes did not spend years trying to track the mastermind down. In October, 1887, at the time of *The Red Headed League*, he had no idea of the existence of Moriarty, yet just over two months later in *The Valley of Fear* he was well aware of him. The only new element was Fred Porlock, who was in any case the invention of the disgruntled detective Athelney Jones, who wished to make a fool of Holmes. But here is Holmes with a totally different version of the tracking of this mastermind, a version that we and Watson know must be false. It is, however, a version which if believed would throw much more credit on the powers of detection of Sherlock Holmes.

Holmes then said he had woven a net around Moriarty and all was ready to close. "In three days, that is to say Monday next ... the Professor, with all the principle members of the gang, will be in the hands of the police." Holmes's problem, however, was surviving until Monday so that he could give evidence later. He claimed that he had been the victim of three attempts upon his life that day. He said there had been a bid to run him down by a horse van, a brick from a rooftop narrowly missed him and on his way to Watson's consulting room he was attacked by 'a rough with a bludgeon'.

These attempts at murder by a master criminal who was 'the Napoleon of crime' and whose agents were 'splendidly organized' seem to be lacking something.

In the first case, that of the horse van, had Holmes in fact been run down there was no guarantee to the would-be murderer that the result would have been fatal - many people have been run down without actually dying from it. The second alleged attempt with a brick from the rooftop was equally unsure. The difficulty of hitting a person moving along the pavement with a brick should not be underestimated. And how the murderer came to put himself on the roof at just the time Holmes was passing is something we can only guess at. The police were not very impressed when Holmes called them in. They found slates and bricks piled on the roof in readiness for some repairs. The official view was that the wind had toppled one of them over. Holmes did not accept it, but it seems far more likely than any other explanation. The last alleged attempt on Holmes's life was the attack by the 'rough'. However, whether it was a murder attempt or not is another matter. If this criminal genius was sending an assassin to kill Holmes in the street, is it likely he would use just one man armed with nothing more than a club?

Surely two or three men with pistols or knives as well as bludgeons would be better able to account for Mr. Holmes? He was, after all, an able exponent of boxing[2] and Japanese wrestling[3] as well as an expert revolver shot. The arch-criminal would doubtless have been aware of Holmes's talents and since Holmes was aware his life was in danger, it was reasonable to assume he was armed and ready to defend himself. He would obviously have been more than a match for a man with a club.

Holmes may well have been attacked, and indeed Watson saw blood on his knuckles, but in the early 1890s London was a violent place and street attacks with robbery as the motive were not uncommon, although they were less frequent than they had been twenty years previously. It is almost certain that the attack on Holmes was a simple attempted robbery.

2) Holmes had boxed at college (*The Gloria Scott*) and was said to be a fine boxer for his weight (*The Yellow Face*). Watson described him as an expert (*The Five Orange Pips* and *A Study in Scarlet*).

3) Holmes defeated Moriarty at the Reichenbach Falls through his knowledge of Baritsu, a Japanese wrestling technique that became popular briefly in the U.K. after it was introduced by E.W. Barton Wright in 1899. It was more properly known as Bartitsu.

Professor Moriarty was not a master criminal. He was not sending people to kill Sherlock Holmes. Holmes had become obsessed with the idea of a 'Napoleon of crime' in 1887. He had been totally convinced by Athelney Jones's practical joke. The idea of a master criminal who was particularly responsible for thwarting Sherlock Holmes was an attractive theory for the detective whose failures were dominating his career.

It was easy for Holmes to justify to himself losing to 'a genius, a philosopher, an abstract thinker' who had a 'brain of the first order'. Even Holmes could swallow that. Being outwitted by a common thief or murderer would be much harder to take.

But what of Professor Moriarty in all this? On this Friday, according to Holmes, Moriarty had called at Baker Street to warn him off. As we have seen, Holmes's reports of events at this time are coloured by his rather special view of what was happening. But let us examine the conversation he claimed took place between them. Moriarty came into the Baker Street sitting room and, after some initial comment, remarked that it is a dangerous habit to 'finger loaded firearms in the pocket of one's dressing gown'. It is a bland comment and when Holmes removed a pistol and laid it cocked upon the table, Moriarty blinked. "You evidently don't know me," he said. The implication in the comment surely is that Holmes would not have bothered with a loaded gun if he had known how harmless his caller was. There followed an exchange of mutual deductions which Holmes may or may not have invented:

Holmes: "I can spare you five minutes if you have anything to say."

Moriarty: "All that I have to say has already crossed your mind."

Holmes: "Then possibly my answer has crossed yours."

Moriarty: "You stand fast?"

Holmes: "Absolutely."

This is really Sherlock Holmes giving Moriarty something of a build-up. Moriarty, it must be remembered, was supposed to be a criminal mastermind. There had been no suggestion that he was Holmes's equal in observation, deduction or mind reading. This is an embellishment.

Moriarty, however, despite the mind reading exchange, still had something he wanted to say to Holmes. It was in the nature of a complaint: "You crossed my path on the 4th of January," he told the detective. "On the 23rd you incommoded me; by the middle of February I was seriously inconvenienced by you; at the end of March I was absolutely hampered in my plans; and now, at the close of April, I find myself placed in such a position through your continual persecution that I am in positive danger of losing my liberty. The situation is becoming an impossible one."

Holmes: "Have you any suggestion to make?"

Moriarty: "You must drop it, Mr. Holmes. You really must you know".

Why Moriarty, the master criminal, should decide it is necessary to warn Holmes off is not clear. Holmes claimed that Moriarty told him: "It would be a grief to me to be forced to take any extreme measure." But in real terms the criminal genius would take whatever steps were necessary. And since Holmes was now, he claimed, in a position to smash the whole of the Professor's organisation, then the only move left would be for the criminal to get Holmes out of the way. But if the Professor's threats are of the same weight as the alleged attempts on Holmes's life, then the consulting detective would not appear to have much to worry about.

Anyway, when he got to Watson, he was already planning to take himself - and the doctor - out of England for a week. "I cannot do better than get away for the few days which remain before the police are at liberty to act." He would, of course, be required for the prosecution, but in the meantime he was better off out of the way.

That is rather a new attitude for Sherlock Holmes. Here was an investigation which he regarded as the summit of his career. Yet he was willing to go off on holiday, leaving it to others to handle the final arrangements for the arrest of the whole gang. This, of course, would be the London police force, whom Holmes had decried as imbeciles time and time again. Surely he would never have left the case - such an important case - in their hands. But apparently he was planning to do just that.

Equally odd is the reason he gave to Watson why Moriarty could not be arrested forthwith: "It would be to ruin the work of three months. We should get the big fish, but the smaller would dart right and left out of the net. On Sunday we should have them all." Would it matter so much that the smaller fish got away? There will, after all, always be minor criminals. It was the organisation's leaders who had to be taken. Holmes may have felt the ideal thing was to root out the whole organisation - but whether it was worth doing it at the cost of his own life is debatable.

But as we have seen, Holmes was behaving distinctly oddly. He claimed he does not want to put Watson in danger, refusing to stay the night because 'you might find me a dangerous guest'. When it came to leaving, Holmes climbed over the back garden wall into Mortimer Street. Now, if Holmes had been followed to Watson's house, his enemies would have seen him enter, but would not have seen him leave. They would have assumed he was still there. Surely that was just as dangerous, if not more dangerous, than staying the night?

Equally, despite not wanting to endanger Watson, Holmes would have been doing just that by taking him to the Continent. But of course there was no real danger.

The pair had arranged to meet the following morning on the Continental Express at Victoria. Watson followed Holmes's instructions that he should send his luggage to Victoria[4], take a cab from his home to the Lowther Arcade, dash through it and at the other end get into a brougham which would be waiting to take him to the station. Watson caught the train and was joined by Holmes, disguised as an Italian priest. But why should Holmes

4) The London railway terminus serving continental boat trains.

find it necessary to be disguised, whereas Watson could arrive at the station quite openly, albeit by a circuitous route? Why should Watson be allowed to send his baggage directly although travelling by a different route? The questions mount up - but the most significant of all is why Holmes thought it necessary to dash to the continent at all.

In fact, there was no need. Holmes did not need to leave the country. But to achieve his objective he had to.

That objective was the death of Professor Moriarty.

Although Holmes had told Watson the whole gang would be arrested on the Monday, Sherlock Holmes was well aware that Professor Moriarty would not be among those charged. There was simply no evidence against him. Neither would the man that Holmes accused of being Moriarty's chief of staff, Colonel Sebastian Moran, be held. Moran's career had been that of an honourable soldier, as Watson was to point out in *The Empty House*. But after his retirement, according to Holmes, he was sought out by Professor Moriarty.

Holmes was to claim, "Moriarty supplied him liberally with money, and used him only in one or two very high class jobs which no ordinary criminal could have undertaken." Why the distinguished retired army officer[5], former big game hunter and occasional author should have wanted to have thrown in with an arch-criminal we shall never know. What we do know is that Holmes had no evidence against him either, and in the event, like Moriarty, he was not arrested.

So who was arrested when the police, on the Monday, acted on Holmes's information? He never makes it clear. One thing that is known is that crime in the capital did not immediately cease. Most likely Holmes had collected information on a number of

---

5)   Colonel Sebastian Moran (born 1840), son of Sir Augustus Moran, a former British Minister to Persia. Educated at Eton and Oxford. Formerly 1st Bengalore Pioneers. Served in Jowaki campaign, Afghan campaign, Charasiab (mentioned in despatches), Sherpur, Cabul. Author of *Heavy Game in the Western Himalayas*, 1881; *Three Months in the Jungle*, 1884. Address: Conduit Street. Clubs: Anglo-Indian; Tankerville; Bagatelle Card Club.

ordinary small-time criminals, claimed they were working for Moriarty and turned evidence of their wrongdoing over to the police. His reason for waiting until the Monday before the arrests were to take place was, as far as the police were concerned, so that Holmes could provide the evidence which would convict Moriarty and Moran. In real terms Holmes had no intention of doing that, He had no evidence against either man. Although they were friends, they were not criminals. That idea existed only in Holmes's fevered brain.

Sherlock Holmes had decided that London without Moriarty would be a better place and so he decided to do away with him. Holmes had always believed he was the final court of appeal. In his career he often showed a tendency not to act against murderers when he had believed they had been justified in taking life. From this it was a short step to deciding that he should take a life himself in what, he was convinced, was the public good.

But how to avoid discovery? He had, after all, made a great deal of fuss about the activities of the Professor. What Holmes did was convince the police that he was going to bring them evidence against Moriarty on the Monday. Meanwhile, he set out to create the illusion that he was being pursued by Moriarty's gang and in fear of his life. Hence the visit to Watson, the dramatic exit over the back garden wall, the account of the various supposed attempts on his life, the circuitous route that Watson had to take to get to Victoria Station and Holmes's news to Watson that morning: "They set fire to our rooms last night. No great harm was done,"

For a master criminal, Moriarty was proving very inefficient.

It was, however, of critical importance that Holmes and Watson caught the Continental Express from Victoria that morning. The reason that Holmes had to get out of England was that he had discovered Moriarty planned a journey to Switzerland. The Professor was not pursuing Holmes - Holmes was pursuing the Professor.

Sherlock Holmes remarked to Watson as the train pulled out

that Moriarty was on the platform having just missed the train. This, however, was nothing more than a further attempt to keep up the illusion that Moriarty was the pursuer. Watson had never seen the Professor and the man pointed out by Holmes could have been anyone. Moriarty, of course, was already aboard the train, as Holmes well knew.

Holmes had learned that Moriarty intended to take a holiday - the Professor probably felt that Sherlock Holmes's 'continual persecution' was getting too much to bear - and what was more, Holmes knew Moriarty's destination. To discover where the Professor intended to spend his holiday would not have been difficult for Sherlock Holmes, any more than it would have been difficult for him to ascertain when Moriarty intended to leave and which train he intended to take.

Nevertheless, Holmes found it necessary to board the train to make sure Moriarty was on it. He needed to be sure that Moriarty had not changed his plans. This would explain why Holmes was in disguise and Watson was not: Moriarty knew Sherlock Holmes, but had never met Dr. Watson.

Holmes, however, did not want to travel in the same train as Moriarty for long. The risk of discovery was too great and he did not want Watson to see a confrontation between himself and the Professor. It was crucial to Holmes's plan that Watson continued to believe that Moriarty was pursuing Holmes in a bid to kill him.

Watson believed - and this is what appeared in *The Final Problem* - that Moriarty in pursuit of Holmes had just missed the train at Victoria. Holmes pretended to deduce that Moriarty would charter a special to chase them and so he and Watson left the boat train at Canterbury. They concealed themselves behind a pile of luggage and saw the special thunder through the station. Watson, of course, thought it contained Moriarty. In fact it was a train hired by Sherlock Holmes.

If Moriarty had just missed the boat train, it would have been impossible for him to charter the special train and for it to be under way in the time available. The boat train, if it had averaged

50 miles an hour, and this was 1891, would have taken about an hour and ten minutes to reach Canterbury from Victoria. Yet the special went through Canterbury Station 'a minute' after Holmes and Watson got out of the boat train. In fact, Watson remarked: "We hardly had time to take our places behind a pile of luggage when it passed."

The special, although it was pulling only one carriage, had made up a vast amount of ground. But even if it had travelled at an average of 75 miles an hour, there would have been only ten minutes available for Moriarty to book the train, for the railway company to have it ready, make sure the line was clear, find a platform, get the engine fired up, get the steam up, Moriarty to get aboard and the train to get under way, That - even with the super-efficient railways of the 1890s - was just not possible. There was not time for Moriarty to book the special and be at Canterbury one minute after the boat train. Moriarty had not, on Watson's account, been aware he would need to catch a train to Dover. Hence he could not have seen the need for the special early enough to have booked it.

The special had, in fact, been booked by Sherlock Holmes considerably earlier. When he and Watson left the express at Canterbury, he was clearly expecting the special to be following. He pretended to deduce that Moriarty would have hired it, but since that was impossible then the deduction must be invalid. Yet Holmes knew the train was coming. The only way he could have known was if he had booked it himself.

Now why should he do that? We can deduce his reason. Getting off the train at Canterbury and letting Watson see the special go by was a master stroke. It totally convinced Watson that they were being hunted by Professor Moriarty and this, as we have seen, was important to Holmes's plan. Second, Holmes needed to see that Moriarty left for Switzerland as he planned and he also needed to keep not too far behind him. The special meant that if by any mischance Watson had missed the express that morning, Holmes still had a means at his disposal of keeping to his schedule.

Holmes had worked out his route well in advance. From Canterbury he and Watson took a slow train via Ashford Junction to Hastings, changed again for Lewes and reached Newhaven at 3.45 that afternoon. They reached Brussels the following Sunday and then via Luxembourg made their way, as Holmes planned, to Switzerland.

On the Monday morning Holmes had telegraphed the police in London, received a reply and 'with a bitter curse hurled it into the grate'.

"I might have known it," he told Watson, "he has escaped."

Indeed he might have known it. Holmes knew quite well that Moriarty was *en route* for Switzerland and well beyond the reach of the London police. Even if the account Watson gave of events was accurate, then Moriarty was on the trail of Holmes and not in London. Holmes had not provided the police with the evidence they would need to arrest Moriarty and they didn't know where he was anyway.

This is again more play-acting to convince Watson, and eventually the public, that things were going badly in Holmes's attempt to put Moriarty in the dock. Holmes, of course, knew where Moriarty was heading, and he and Watson spent 'a charming week' wandering up the Valley of the Rhône before making their way, via Interlaken, to Meiringen, the little village that lies in the shadow of the Reichenbach Falls - for this 'fearful place' where the 'torrent ... plunges into a tremendous abyss' was where Sherlock Holmes had decided that Professor James Moriarty was to meet his death.

All of this time Moriarty had merely been enjoying a holiday in Switzerland in company with his friend, Colonel Sebastian Moran. It would have been doubly peaceful for the Professor since he would have felt that he had left Holmes behind him in London. The academic and the old soldier would have walked in the hills around Meiringen and Rosenlaui, enjoying the Alpine air and scenery and may even have visited the falls at Reichenbach before the fatal encounter.

Holmes, of course, knew exactly where Moriarty was all this time. He had known the Professor's destination from the very start and had confirmed that he was really on his way there. But how did he manage to lure Professor Moriarty to the falls ... and his death?

Why would Moriarty go to the Reichenbach Falls alone? As we know from *The Empty House*, Holmes claimed Moriarty had accomplices with him, but they were not near enough to save the Professor from his fate. Why on earth, if he was really a master criminal bent on sending Holmes to his death, did he go alone? Why not turn up with as many accomplices as would be necessary to do the deed? And why not use firearms? Or if silence was necessary, knives or clubs. Why should Moriarty engage in a hand to hand fight to the death in such a place?

The answer, of course, is that he had no such intention. Moriarty was lured to the Reichenbach Falls, just as Watson was lured away, with a fake letter written by Sherlock Holmes. The letter to Moriarty must have played on the thing that troubled him most, the continual persecution by Sherlock Holmes. Perhaps it warned of danger and offered some help. We shall never know the detail of the note, but the condition must have been a meeting above the falls alone. The Professor, it seems, accepted the letter as genuine, but although he went by himself, arranged that his friend Moran should remain in the vicinity.

Watson meanwhile had been tricked into going back to his hotel, leaving Holmes at the falls. Here again we see that Holmes was determined to remain there on his own. Watson got a letter purporting to call him back to the hotel in Meiringen to attend an English woman who was 'in the last stage of consumption' and wanted an English doctor. Of course, he had to interrupt his walk and go. But why leave Holmes? The pair had been planning to walk from Meiringen to the nearby hamlet of Rosenlaui. Surely most people under the circumstances would have returned together to Meiringen and made the expedition to Rosenlaui another day. They were ostensibly on holiday, after all. But they decided not to do this. Watson was to return to Meiringen and Holmes intended to continue on to Rosenlaui. It seems a very unlikely way for two friends on holiday together to go on.

However, Watson was soon out of the way, leaving Holmes with the Swiss lad who had brought Watson's bogus letter. No doubt the same lad had taken the other fake letter to Professor Moriarty, Holmes now had everybody in the right place for the events that were to follow. Watson on his way to Meiringen, to learn his letter was a fake; Moriarty hurrying to Reichenbach for a meeting alone with someone who could help him escape the attentions of Holmes; the Swiss lad would have been paid off soon after Watson left, leaving Sherlock Holmes alone at the Reichenbach Falls awaiting Professor Moriarty.

Holmes, of course, had been playing up the attempts on his life right until the last, Watson reports in *The Final Problem* "as we passed over the Gemmi ... a large rock which had been dislodged from the ridge upon our right clattered down and roared into the lake behind us. In an instant Holmes had raced up on to the ridge and ... craned his neck in every direction".

The guide pointed out, quite rightly, that a fall of stones was a common chance in the spring time at that spot, but Holmes was apparently unconvinced. He knew a Moriarty when he saw one. However, he said nothing, 'but he smiled at me with the air of a man who sees the fulfilment of that which he had expected'.

The way was prepared, but, as so often in the past, Sherlock Holmes had blundered, he was about to commit the cold-blooded and premeditated murder of a distinguished scientist. But there was going to be a witness.

Professor Moriarty, although sticking to the conditions set out in the bogus letter, and going alone to his appointment with death, had taken one precaution. He had sent his companion, Colonel Moran, to a point above the path from where he would be able to see all that went on. Holmes had not counted on this. He had expected that his interview with Moriarty would be absolutely private. The sound of the falling water would drown any shout for help and there was only one way up to the vantage point. Holmes had not expected to be disturbed at his work.

He must have kept out of sight, flattened against the rock wall until Moriarty was almost upon him. Then it would have taken but a moment for Holmes to grab the Professor, apply an armlock and hurl him over the precipice.

It was over. Sherlock Holmes had taken the law into his own hands, acted as judge, jury and executioner and accounted for the man he thought had controlled a vast criminal empire. But it was far from being a perfect result. A rock displaced from above revealed that there had been a witness to the crime, the distinguished big game hunter and former soldier, Sebastian Moran. What could Holmes do? Moran would most likely alert the police and have the detective arrested for murder. Holmes had to make good his getaway, and he had to cloud the issue sufficiently that Watson would continue to defend him. He therefore tore three pages from his notebook and wrote the note to Watson which appeared in *The Final Problem*. It was a letter designed to do two things: to convince Watson and the authorities that Holmes had died in the Reichenbach Falls and also to further show the world that Moriarty was, in fact, the criminal mastermind that Holmes claimed. It succeeded in both aims.

There was, however, an investigation. Obviously the police had to be brought into the matter, but Watson's story would have convinced them that Moriarty was the 'Napoleon of crime'. The letter indicated that Holmes was left alone with Moriarty and an examination of the footmarks on the path left them in no doubt that both men had plunged to their deaths. We know, of course, that Sherlock Holmes survived, so this examination cannot have been quite as exhaustive as it might have been.

If there had been no witness to the death of Moriarty, then Holmes would have simply returned to the hotel at Meiringen and told Watson and possibly the police that he had been ambushed by his enemy and that the enemy had unfortunately perished. The evidence of the faked letter which took Watson back to Meiringen would have been sufficient to convince all but the most obstinate policeman that Holmes had escaped another attempt on his life. Had circumstances permitted it, Holmes may even have decided not to bring the police into the affair.

But of course there had been a witness. Colonel Moran may have been accused by Holmes of being Moriarty's chief of staff, but nothing had ever been proved against him, or the Professor. He may have claimed Holmes was still alive, but there was considerable doubt. Holmes, as we know, did not turn up again for a matter of some three years.

Sherlock Holmes had made good his escape from the Reichenbach Falls by climbing up the rockface from the end of the path where he had fought Moriarty. This climb, towards the place from where Moran had witnessed the death struggle, meant that Holmes would have avoided meeting anyone coming up the path. Watson would have already started back to the falls having discovered he had been lured away by a bogus letter, and Moran had dashed away to alert the police to the murder. Sherlock Holmes, who was now supposed to be dead, could hardly afford to be seen by Watson, or a posse of policeman, as he descended the path from the falls.

The inquiry into the deaths of Moriarty and Sherlock Holmes at Reichenbach would have been faced with two opposing versions of the events.

On the one hand, there was Colonel Moran's story that Professor Moriarty, an innocent academic, had been the subject of persecution by Sherlock Holmes, who was under the mistaken impression that the Professor was a criminal mastermind. Moran would have told the police that things had reached such a pitch that Moriarty had gone to Holmes in London and asked him to stop. Holmes had refused and Moriarty had decided the best thing to do was to take a holiday on the Continent in order to get away from Holmes's attentions. Colonel Moran, an old friend of the Professor, had agreed to accompany him. Moran would have recounted for the police that a letter asking the Professor to the meeting at the Reichenbach Falls and mentioning Sherlock Holmes had been received by the Professor. Moriarty had decided to keep the appointment because he was eager for any help in convincing Holmes that he was nothing more than a mathematician. Moran had climbed to a vantage point overlooking the path where the meeting was to take place so that he could see what went on. To his horror, as the Professor approached, Moran saw Sherlock Holmes - who had apparently followed them from England - step from the rockface, seize Moriarty by the arm and hurl him into the abyss. Moran then dashed down the mountain to report to the police what he had seen.

The police would have made inquiries about Colonel Moran. They would have discovered that he was a retired Indian army officer with a distinguished career, a successful big game hunter and the author of two books on the subject. He lived in London, was a member of a number of clubs and was an old friend of Professor Moriarty. In all, he was highly respectable and nothing was known against him.

The second version of the affair would have been Dr. Watson's. He would have told the police that Sherlock Holmes had been working on a case which would have established that Professor Moriarty controlled a vast criminal empire. Holmes's life had been in danger every hour he remained in London. There had been three attempts to kill him the day before they left. The rooms in Baker Street had been set on fire in yet another murder bid, and as the pair caught the boat train, Holmes had seen Moriarty just miss it. This was confirmed when Watson saw the special train which he believed Moriarty had chartered so that he could continue pursuing Holmes. Watson would have remembered the rock fall at Gemmi and would have been able to show the police the fake letter which had lured him back to Meiringen, leaving Holmes at the Reichenbach Falls.

The Swiss police would, no doubt, have contacted the London police, who would have confirmed that Holmes had been working on the case against Moriarty and his gang. They would have said that a number of the gang had been arrested, but that they were still waiting for evidence against Moriarty and Colonel Moran. They would have told the Swiss police that in January, 1887, some three years earlier, Holmes had told Inspector MacDonald that Moran was Moriarty's chief of staff at a salary of six thousand pounds a year.

At the scene of the crime they found the footprints which, as Watson reports, were examined by an expert, who concluded both Moriarty and Holmes must have perished. There was the note which Holmes left for Watson under his cigarette case and which Watson found when he returned to the falls after discovering that the letter calling him back to the hotel was a fake.

"My dear Watson," Holmes had written, "I write these few lines through the courtesy of Mr. Moriarty, who awaits my convenience for the final discussion of those questions which lie between us. He has been giving me a sketch of the methods by which he avoided the English police and kept himself informed of our movements. They certainly confirm the very high opinion which I had formed of his abilities. I am pleased to think that I shall he able to free society from any further effects of his presence, though I fear that it is at a cost which will give pain to my friends and especially, my dear Watson, to you. I have already explained to you, however, that my career had in any case reached its crisis, and that no possible conclusion to it could be more congenial to me than this. Indeed, if I may make a full confession to you, I was quite convinced that the letter from Meiringen was a hoax, and I allowed you to depart on that errand under the persuasion that some development of this sort would follow. Tell Inspector Patterson that the papers which he needs to convict the gang are in pigeon-hole M, done up in a blue envelope and inscribed 'Moriarty'. I made every disposition of my property before leaving England, and handed it to my brother Mycroft. Pray give my greetings to Mrs. Watson, and believe me to be my dear fellow, Very sincerely yours, Sherlock Holmes."

This letter clearly indicated that Moriarty was waiting for Holmes with murderous intent and that Holmes, at least, still believed Moriarty to be a criminal genius.

Last, there was the absence of Sherlock Holmes. He had completely disappeared. Watson had hurried back to the falls after being lured back to the hotel and he had not met Holmes coming down. As he remarked in *The Empty House*, 'there were two sets of tracks going down the path and none returning'. Everything pointed to Holmes and Moriarty both having met their deaths in the falls,

Against this, there was the evidence of Colonel Moran. He claimed he had seen Holmes throw Moriarty over and he further claimed Holmes had survived. In that case, where was Sherlock Holmes?

As far as the Swiss police were concerned they had one eyewitness, Colonel Moran, against whom there was nothing known. Then they had Dr. Watson's testimony and again he was a respectable man. The circumstantial evidence tended to support Watson's view of things. However, if Sherlock Holmes had survived, things would have been very different. First, it would have given enough credibility to Colonel Moran's version of things that the police would have had to look far more deeply into the affair. Sherlock Holmes alive would have been forced to produce the evidence he had promised that Moriarty really was a master criminal. Dead, he was obviously unable to do so.

Once it was clear that Moran had seen what happened, it was obvious that Holmes had to appear to be dead. Had Moran not been a witness then Holmes would have been able to return from the falls with the story of a murderous attack on him by the evil Professor who had been pursuing him throughout Europe. He would have been able to claim that in the struggle the villain had fallen from the path to his death. Watson would have supported all of Holmes's claims about how Moriarty had been chasing them. Moran would have denied it all, of course, but Holmes would have included him in the smear. Since Moran had seen what went on, had seen Holmes throw Moriarty over and had rushed to the police to report it, Holmes was in some difficulty. He would be accused of murder and would have had to defend himself against it. That would have been a far different story.

As far as the Swiss police were concerned, since both foreign nationals were dead the affair had, in real terms, resolved itself. All they had to do was keep the file open should any new details emerge later and send a report to the Foreign Office in London.

Sherlock Holmes and Professor Moriarty were both officially dead.

Colonel Sebastian Moran, who witnessed Sherlock Holmes throw Professor Moriarty to his death at the Reichenbach Falls.

CHAPTER TEN

The Authorised Version

Sherlock Holmes clearly did not want to find himself charged with murder. He had no evidence against Moriarty and was taking the law into his own hands by following him to Switzerland and killing him. The only witness to what had happened above the Reichenbach Falls was Colonel Moran, and Holmes had no evidence to blacken his name either. The only way that Holmes' version of Moriarty's death could be credible was if Holmes himself were dead.

But Sherlock Holmes was alive. Colonel Moran was aware of what had really happened, but as long as the authorities thought Sherlock Holmes had died along with Moriarty, Moran's account was overshadowed by the weight of evidence on Holmes's side. However, were Holmes to reappear then it could be that some rather awkward questions would have to be answered.

At this time only two people knew what had really happened at the Reichenbach Falls: Sherlock Holmes himself and Colonel Moran. But Holmes, who by his own account, made off over the mountains to Florence in northern Italy[1] after Moriarty was killed, was soon to let another person know that he was still alive. He told Watson in *The Empty House* that he had to confide in his brother Mycroft in order to obtain the money he needed.

Watson, of course, said that Sherlock Holmes reappeared in 1894. He called on Watson in that year disguised as an elderly bookseller, causing Watson to faint 'for the first and last time' in

1) W.S. Baring-Gould has speculated in his biography of Sherlock Holmes that Holmes went to Montenegro where he had a liaison with Irene Adler. Miss Adler had discovered that her marriage to Norton had been conducted by a bogus priest. Norton, according to this theory, had been a brutal fortune-hunter. Baring-Gould contends the affair took place in June, 1891, and that a child was born as a result. Baring-Gould has identified the child as the well-known New York detective, Nero Wolfe.

his life. But was Watson really still unaware at this time that Holmes had survived? Could it not be that to save further explanation he merely invented Holmes's dramatic reappearance?

Holmes's reason for his absence was that 'the instant the Professor disappeared (over the precipice) it struck me what a really extraordinarily lucky chance Fate had placed in my way'.

Holmes claimed that Moriarty was not the only man who had sworn his death. There were at least three others and, claimed Holmes, sooner or later one or the other would get him. But if the whole world believed him to be dead, these men would 'take liberties' and sooner or later lay themselves open so that Holmes could destroy them.

However, whether Watson heard that explanation in April, 1894, or soon after Holmes's disappearance in May, 1891, is a matter for debate.

We know that Mycroft knew Sherlock was still alive. But would Mycroft have swallowed Holmes's explanation? Mycroft, after all, would have seen all the official papers on the case and, as Sherlock had admitted much earlier, he possessed powers of observation and deduction 'in a larger degree' than Sherlock Holmes. It would have been quite clear to Mycroft that Sherlock's story was a fabrication. He would have realised that his brother had travelled to Switzerland in order to murder the Professor. Whether he would have accepted Sherlock's assertion that James Moriarty was a criminal is another matter. Mycroft would have seen that there was no evidence to support the accusation, but may have accepted his brother's word for it and felt that the extermination of Moriarty, if he was all that Sherlock claimed, was a matter of public interest. In any event he agreed to help.

The question, of course, was how they could rehabilitate Sherlock Holmes into society. If he suddenly reappeared he was going to have to have a very good story. His appearance alive and well would give a lot of weight to Colonel Moran's version of what had occurred at Reichenbach.

While Mycroft pondered the problem, Sherlock, under an assumed name, went round the world[2]. "I travelled for two years in Tibet, therefore, and amused myself by visiting Lhassa[3] and spending some days with the head lama ... I then passed through Persia, looked in at Mecca, and paid a short, but interesting, visit to the Khalifa at Khartoum, the results of which I have communicated to the Foreign Office[4]. Returning to France, I spent some months in a research into the coal-tar derivatives, which I conducted in a laboratory in Montpelier ..."

Did Mycroft tell Watson that Sherlock was still alive? The answer has to be that he must have. Mycroft, as we know, arranged for the upkeep of the Baker Street rooms throughout this period. Watson, with a practice in Kensington[5], may not have regularly visited 221B, but he would certainly have been more than a little puzzled had he visited Mrs. Hudson to discover that the old rooms were being maintained just as before. Mycroft could hardly have sworn Mrs. Hudson to secrecy and she would have admitted that the rooms were being paid for by Sherlock Holmes's brother. Watson would have wondered why and would no doubt have asked Mycroft. Mrs. Hudson would also have wondered why. Perhaps she asked as well.

In any event, Mycroft could hardly have taken the chance of Watson just happening to find out and then giving the game away. Whatever explanation he gave Watson for Holmes's absence - and

2) During his absence from England Sherlock Holmes may have been acting as an agent for the British Government. (*Sherlock Holmes's Wanderjahre*, A. Carson Simpson, Philadelphia 1953-1956. Four vols.)

3) Holmes may have investigated the phenomena of the 'abominable snowman' while in Tibet. (*On the Remarkable Explorations of Sigerson*, Winifred M. Christie. *Sherlock Holmes Journal*, September, 1952).

4) The Khalifa was in residence at Omdurman in 1893, but this would not have prevented a meeting at Khartoum, scene of the massacre of General Gordon and his troops some eight years earlier. The Foreign Office would doubtless have been interested in intelligence from the area and this may have contributed to General Kitchener's expedition in 1898 when the Khalifa was overthrown.

5) Dr Watson had sold his Paddington practice in June, 1891, and re-purchased his former practice in Kensington.

it is probably the explanation that Watson attributes to Holmes in *The Empty House*: that if he was thought dead his remaining enemies would 'take liberties' - Mycroft must have told Watson that Holmes was alive and lying low. Watson, therefore, and maybe even Mrs. Hudson, would have been involved in the plan to bring Sherlock Holmes back in such a way that no taint of scandal would result from the death of Professor Moriarty,

How they managed it is clear from the publication dates of the stories of Sherlock Holmes. He had first appeared in *A Study in Scarlet* which was published in 1887 in *Beeton's Christmas Annual*; Holmes next appeared in *The Sign of Four* in *Lippincott's Magazine* in February, 1890. These two stories, which achieved a modest degree of success, gave Mycroft the clue to rehabilitating his brother. A meeting of Sherlock, Mycroft and Watson must have been arranged shortly after Sherlock's disappearance when it was decided that the details of Sherlock's cases, which Watson had been writing up, should be published and that Sherlock Holmes's name - already fairly well-known as a result of the two stories already published - should be publicised until it was a household word.

The stories would show Sherlock Holmes as a confidant of the rich, powerful and influential people who were his clients. The first appeared in the *Strand Magazine* in July, 1891, only eight weeks after Holmes had disappeared, and was an overnight success. It was *A Scandal in Bohemia* and showed Holmes acting for a king.

This was followed that August by *The Red Headed League*; in September there was *A Case of Identity* and thereafter the stories appeared monthly until June of the following year. They were a huge success and George Newnes brought out a collected edition in London that year and Harper Bros. published the same collection in New York. In December of that year the *Strand Magazine* began a new series of a dozen stories about Sherlock Holmes. In America all of these stories, with the exception of the last, were published in *Harper's Weekly*. Sherlock Holmes's name had become known throughout the world.

The campaign was a resounding success. Mycroft, whose idea it had been in the first instance, he having perceived the interest that there had been in the two early stories about Holmes, was delighted. Watson's pleasure at the success of the stories would have been immeasurable, since the money they earned gave him, for the first time, a degree of financial security. The success of the Sherlock Holmes stories would also have given great satisfaction to another man.

Like Watson, Arthur Conan Doyle was a doctor. He was born in 1859, joined the medical faculty of Edinburgh University in 1876, interrupting his studies to sign on a whaling ship which took him to the Arctic and back, and, when qualified, he returned to the sea as the surgeon on a passenger liner to West Africa. Doyle, like Watson, had travelled the world, although not as extensively as his fellow doctor. His graduation and appointment as ship's surgeon took place in 1881, the year that Watson moved to Baker Street, Doyle was doubtless in London for a time during that year and Watson, who had yet to become a close friend of Holmes although they shared an apartment, was still in the habit of passing his time fairly aimlessly.

The two men were introduced. Perhaps by a fellow doctor, perhaps by Watson's old friend Stamford. They may even have met in the Criterion Bar, although it could well have been somewhere cheaper. The two became friends, although they were to meet only infrequently. Doyle went back to sea for a brief spell and then joined an old friend in a practice in Plymouth. The partnership did not last, however, and Doyle left for Southsea, near Portsmouth, where he set up his own practice. He had always had an interest in writing and while at medical school had earned three guineas from *Chambers' Journal* for a short story called *The Mystery of Sasassa Valley* He had sent in some stories after this, but all had been rejected. In Southsea his practice did not occupy him full time and he again turned his hand to writing.

In 1883 the prestigious *Cornhill Magazine* had accepted his story *J. Habakuk Jephson's Statement* and although much of his work continued to be rejected, he made a start on his first novel, *Girdlestone & Co.* He was confident enough, however, to take a wife. Dr. Watson was one of the guests at the wedding and thereafter would visit Doyle and his family at Southsea once or twice a year. In *The Cardboard Box*, which took place in September, 1889, Watson remarked how he 'yearned for the glades of the New Forest or the shingle of Southsea'. By then his visits to the Doyle family had become a regular part of his life.

Arthur Conan Doyle had been intrigued by Watson's description of the strange detective with whom he shared rooms and had compared him with his old instructor at Edinburgh, Dr. Joseph Bell, who had a similar capacity for observation and deduction, although to a far lesser degree. It was during one visit to Southsea in 1885 that Doyle suggested to Watson that he should set down some of his reminiscences in story form. Watson, who had no ambition in a literary direction, demurred, but was fired by Doyle's enthusiasm for the project. In the end he agreed on a collaboration and so he related the affair called *A Study in Scarlet*. Doyle put it down in basic form and the two men worked together on the story until it was considered finished.

They agreed to split the proceeds, but because Doyle's name was better known as a writer decided that he should appear as the author. Watson's credit came in the sub-heading: *Being a reprint from the Reminiscences of John H. Watson, M.D., Late of the Army Medical Department.*

The story was accepted for the 1887 edition of *Beeton's Christmas Annual*. The fee, for the outright sale of the copyright, was £25. It created no sensation and both Doyle and Watson continued their lives as before, each £12. 10s. 0d. (£12.50) richer. In 1889 they were to collaborate again. The American editor of *Lippincott's Magazine* asked Doyle for a new novel about Sherlock Holmes. The two men worked on the book that July and it was published in February, 1890, simultaneously in England and the United States. In August, 1889, that Watson yearned for the shingle of Southsea. He felt unable to impose himself on the Doyles again and, in any case, following his recent marriage, he had to work for a living. His bank balance was, in his own word, depleted, since he had bought a medical practice in Paddington and it was necessary for him to work to build it up.

Both men had done well out of *The Sign of Four*, Watson using part of the proceeds to buy his practice and Doyle using his share, together with earnings from other writings, to give up the Southsea practice and work full time as a writer.

The stories that were published during Sherlock Holmes's absence from London made both Doyle and Watson financially secure. Doyle, of course, took an extra share of the earnings since he was also handling all the business arrangements and acting as agent. But although this was part of his function, he was never merely the agent and he was never merely a kind of ghost writer. His collaboration with Watson was one in which both men gave equally to the form, style and writing of the stories.

Doyle eventually became disenchanted with Sherlock Holmes as a character, and considered the Sherlock Holmes stories were interfering with his other more serious work. It may have been that he was keen to get away from a character that he had not actually created. Nevertheless, he and Watson were to continue writing together until 1927[6].

The success of the Sherlock Holmes stories led to a great deal of theatrical interest. Holmes and Watson were first portrayed on the stage of London's Royal Court Theatre in 1893 in a playlet, part of a triple bill, called *Under the Clock*. Holmes was played by the actor Charles Brookfield, who had written the piece with Seymour Hicks, playing Watson. The next year Charles Rogers's drama *Sherlock Holmes*, with John Webb as Holmes and St. John Hamund as Watson, went on in London. Doubtless Watson, Mycroft Holmes and Arthur Conan Doyle were in the first night audience. Sherlock Holmes, of course, was still languishing in

6) Their last collaboration was *The Adventure of Shoscombe Old Place*, which was first published in March, 1927.

France, awaiting an opportunity to return to London.

Only one thing remained before he could return: the authorised version of the death of Moriarty had to be presented to the public. Consequently Watson once more took up his pen to 'write the last words by which I shall record the singular gifts' of Sherlock Holmes. There followed the version of the affair which was to gain universal acceptance. The evil Professor had pursued Holmes to Switzerland and died at the Reichenbach Falls as he attempted to throw Holmes over. Holmes had gallantly given his life to free London from Moriarty's stranglehold.

The death of Holmes, even though published so long after the supposed event, brought a period of near national mourning. The whole thing had been a total success. Sherlock Holmes was free to return to London and his Baker Street rooms, yet the public would not hear of him again until 1901[7] and it would not be revealed in print that he had escaped the Reichenbach Falls until October, 1903.

Meanwhile Sherlock Holmes, who the world thought dead, could once more practice as a detective. And he could do it in almost complete anonymity.

The young Doctor Stamford.

---

7) *The Hound of the Baskervilles* was serialised in the *Strand* magazine commencing August, 1901.

CHAPTER ELEVEN

The Second Victim

Who killed the Honourable Ronald Adair? The second son of the Earl of Maynooth was shot dead in his sitting room at the house in Park Lane which he shared with his mother and sister on the night of 30th March, 1894.

Sherlock Holmes had no doubt who the killer was. Shortly before his death, Adair had been playing whist at the Bagatalle Card Club and his partner had been none other than Colonel Sebastian Moran.

But why should Moran have wanted to kill the young aristocrat? He and Adair regularly played cards together and there was no evidence of any animosity between them.

Holmes's answer - which he admitted to be conjecture - was that Adair had discovered Moran cheating at cards and given him an ultimatum: he must resign from his clubs[1] and undertake never to play cards again. If he refused, then Adair would expose him. According to Holmes's theory, Moran was at that time living on his winnings from card playing and therefore was unable to comply without impoverishing himself. To avoid being exposed as a cheat, he had shot dead his accuser.

There is no evidence to suggest that Holmes's guess was correct, but Moran was found in possession of the murder weapon and this, coupled with his association with Adair, was damning evidence.

But was Moran the killer of Adair? And if not, who was? Could there have been more, much more, to the case than Sherlock Holmes ever revealed? It is certainly strange that Holmes's return to London after his long absence following the

---

1) His clubs were: The Anglo-Indian; the Tankerville; and the Bagatelle Card Club.

The Hon. Ronald Adair, murdered by Sherlock Holmes in 1894.

death of Professor Moriarty coincided with the death of another friend of Colonel Moran.

The Adair murder, Watson recounted in *The Empty House*, had absorbed all London and dismayed the fashionable world. Watson, unaware that Sherlock Holmes had returned, was taking an interest in the case himself, and had visited Park Lane to look at the outside of the house in which the shooting had taken place.

Adair had been found alone in the room with a head wound caused by an expanding bullet. The door had been locked on the inside, but because there was no weapon in the room it was clear that the shot had been fired through the window.

While Watson was turning the mystery over in his mind, Holmes made his reappearance, calling on the doctor in the guise of an elderly bookseller. Sherlock Holmes claimed that he returned from France after hearing about the Adair murder. It is, however, clear that he had something else on his mind. He took Watson by cab to Cavendish Square from where they made their way, taking alleyways rather than the main roads, to Camden House, which was empty and stood opposite 221B Baker Street.

Looking up at the window of their old rooms, Watson was somewhat surprised to see the familiar profile of Sherlock Holmes thrown as a silhouette on the blind. Holmes had set up a wax bust of himself so that he appeared to be in the apartment.

Sherlock Holmes told Watson he was waiting for 'the most dangerous and cunning criminal in London', Professor Moriarty's former chief of staff. He had set a trap for Colonel Moran.

Moran, of course, was the one man, other than Sherlock Holmes, who knew the truth about how Professor Moriarty met his death at the Reichenbach Falls. He also knew that there was no foundation to Holmes' claims that Professor Moriarty was an arch-criminal, but he had little hope of convincing the authorities of it. Watson's published version of the affair had been as readily accepted by the public as his other accounts of Sherlock Holmes's adventures. The distinguished Professor Moriarty's posthumous reputation had been totally blackened. In death he had become 'the Napoleon of crime'.

But Moran, the old soldier and famous tiger hunter, had vowed that his friend's death should not go unavenged; he intended that Holmes should pay for murdering the Professor.

And so, as Holmes and Watson waited in the darkness in Camden House, they heard the sounds of someone entering. Colonel Moran set up a gun at the window, aiming at the silhouette of Holmes opposite. There was a brief struggle and Moran was captured. The police, led by Inspector Lestrade, had been waiting a short distance away and were soon on the scene.

But what was Moran to be charged with? The attempted murder of Sherlock Holmes? "Not so," Holmes told the inspector. "I do not propose to appear in the matter at all." Holmes advised Lestrade to have the weapon that Moran was using examined. It was a powerful airgun and, Holmes said, was the weapon that killed Ronald Adair.

Moran had a great deal of explaining to do. He knew Adair well and often played cards with him. There was the 'cheating' theory as a motive, and now Moran had been caught trying to kill Holmes with the gun that killed Adair. Moran was arrested and Sherlock Holmes's trap had sprung on the only witness to the murder at Reichenbach Falls.

But what kind of trap? Certainly Holmes set up the wax bust of himself in the Baker street rooms and waited for Moran to arrive and take a shot at it. But was that the extent of the ruse?

How, for example, did Holmes know that Moran was going to come at that particular time? And, for that matter, how did Moran know that Holmes was back in London? Even Watson was unaware he had returned and Holmes was definitely not advertising the fact. He was, after all, going about in an elaborate disguise. If Moran was simply a private individual bent on revenge, he had no way of knowing that Holmes, after three years of wandering round the world, had secretly returned to London. Holmes's impressions of Moran were somewhat contradictory. In *The Empty House* he told Watson that Moran was 'the most dangerous and cunning criminal in London'. But once the case was cleared up, he revealed that he suspected Moran made his living playing cards. A cardsharp would have no more opportunity than a private individual of learning that Holmes was back. As to a dangerous and cunning criminal, even had he been the former chief of staff of the 'Moriarty gang' - which he was not - he would have had problems in keeping track of Holmes for three years. It would have been even more difficult since, according to Holmes, the gang had been smashed in 1891. There had been nothing left of it.

The only way that Moran could have learned Sherlock Holmes was back in London was if someone had told him. And since Holmes had been keeping his return secret, there would have been few people who knew. The person who told Moran must also have indicated that Holmes would be in Baker Street for a limited period, perhaps just the night. Otherwise how could Holmes have been sure Moran would turn up while he was there with Watson? This means that Holmes must have been aware of the extent of Moran's information. Sherlock Holmes knew what Moran had been told.

It was Holmes who was trying to trap Moran and it was Holmes who decided when he would put the target in the Baker Street window. Yet the information which reached Moran was accurate and must, therefore, have come from Sherlock Holmes.

Either in disguise, or using an intermediary, Holmes had been in contact with Colonel Moran prior to the arrest in Camden House. He had lured the Colonel to Baker Street. Holmes knew that with Moran free in London, his own life would not be worth living. "Night and day the shadow would have been over me, and sooner or later, his chance must have come." Sherlock Holmes had been after Moran ever since the death of Moriarty. "I read the papers with some attention during my sojourn in France, on the lookout for my chance of laying him by the heels."

But just how far did Sherlock Holmes go in trying to rid himself of Moran? Could he have tried to frame the Colonel for the Adair killing?

The key to the whole thing must be the airgun. There is no doubt that this was the weapon which had killed Ronald Adair. Holmes's assertion that it was the same gun would have been easily checked by scientific methods even in 1894.

Moran was therefore caught with the weapon used in the Adair murder in his hands. If he did not kill Ronald Adair, where did he get the gun from? Significantly Sherlock Holmes was obviously familiar with the airgun[2]. Immediately after Moran was arrested, Holmes was able to say that the gun had been built by the blind German mechanic Von Herder. It should be recalled that in 1891 when Holmes went to Watson's house to ask him to go to the continent - the trip that led to the death of Professor Moriarty - Holmes claimed that he was afraid an attempt would be made on his life with an airgun. We know, of course, that Holmes's claim that his life was in danger at that time was not true - it was merely a device to convince Watson, and later the world, that Moriarty was a dangerous criminal. Nobody was pursuing Holmes with an airgun then, any more than the 'rough' who had attacked Holmes with a bludgeon three years before was an assassin in Moriarty's pay.

Yet by 1894 Moran had acquired a high-powered airgun and was prepared to use it to kill Holmes in revenge for the death of the Professor. It surely cannot be coincidence. So where did Moran get the gun?

Is it possible that Holmes used his underworld contacts to obtain the weapon which had been used to murder Adair, had let the real killer go, and had then introduced the gun to Moran. It was, after all, a powerful and silent weapon, ideal for Moran's intended revenge killing.

---

2)   Holmes claimed the gun had been made by the blind German mechanic Von Herder at the instructions of Professor Moriarty. By picking it up at the scene of the crime Sherlock Holmes made sure his own fingerprints were on the weapon. Scotland Yard did not start using fingerprint identification until 1901, but the system was already well known.

It is just about feasible that Sherlock Holmes could have obtained the gun and then got it into Moran's hands. But it is surely too much of a coincidence that the weapon should have been an airgun, the very type of gun that Holmes had mentioned three years earlier.

But it is possible that Sherlock Holmes could have been in possession of the gun which killed Ronald Adair, and it could have been an airgun ... *if the murderer of Adair had been Sherlock Holmes.*

But why should Holmes want to kill Adair? According to Watson's account, the young aristocrat 'moved in the best society, had, so far as was known, no enemies and no particular vices'.

The reason is that Sherlock Holmes, still suffering from the delusion that Moriarty and Moran had headed a vast criminal empire, had identified Adair as another member of the gang.

In *The Empty House*, before Moran was arrested, Holmes told Watson that the trial 'of the Moriarty gang left two of its most dangerous members, my own most vindictive enemies, at liberty'. One of those enemies was clearly Colonel Moran; the other was Ronald Adair.

We know, of course, that there had been no 'Moriarty gang' and that the trial Holmes referred to was that of a number of small-time crooks against whom Holmes had been able to provide evidence of criminal activity. But why did he think Adair was part of Moriarty's empire?

The answer is that Adair was a known associate of Sebastian Moran. The two men regularly played cards together, partnering each other at whist. Some weeks before his death, Adair had won £420 in a sitting when he was partnered by Moran. Holmes, still bent on wiping out the last remnants of what he considered was Moriarty's gang, decided to kill two birds with one stone. He had probably been in possession of the Von Herder airgun for some years. It is almost certainly the weapon he referred to in 1891. With it he shot Adair through the open window of his room. It was an act which would have troubled his conscience no more than the killing of Moriarty.

Holmes, who we know had been in contact with Moran before the Colonel's arrest, would then have organised the tip-off that Holmes would be back in Baker Street on a certain evening. No doubt he did this himself, using one of his many highly-effective disguises. At the same time, he would have offered the airgun as the ideal weapon for Moran to carry out the killing. If Moran used one of his own sporting rifles, there was a chance it could be traced and in any event such a weapon would be difficult to carry around unobtrusively. It would also be noisy and could well lead to a hue and cry. The airgun meanwhile was silent and quite small. It would also add a touch of poetic justice since Watson, in his account of *The Final Problem*, which had been published only four months earlier, had quoted Holmes as saying he was afraid of airguns.

Once Moran accepted the gun, the matter was settled. Even if he had decided subsequently to use some other weapon for his attempt on Sherlock Holmes's life, he was still going to be arrested because Holmes knew when and where he would make the attempt. Once Moran was held, a police search of his rooms would have revealed the weapon used in the Adair murder. However, as we know, Moran took the airgun to Baker Street with him and it was quickly identified by Holmes as the weapon used to murder Ronald Adair.

When he was arrested Moran suddenly realised that he had walked into a trap. Without being told, he knew that the gun he held in his hands, the gun he had been so lucky to acquire, was the one which had been used to kill his friend Ronald Adair.

Sherlock Holmes had wanted Adair out of the way, just as he had wanted Moriarty out of the way, and he had been successful. Now Moran faced the rope for the Adair murder. "You cunning, cunning fiend," Moran told Holmes. "You clever, clever fiend."

But the trap, no matter how carefully it had been set, failed in the end. Moran did not go to the gallows. He was acquitted of the Adair murder. No record of the trial remains, but in 1902

Holmes referred to the 'living Colonel Sebastian Moran' as a highly dangerous criminal[3]. Clearly if he had been found guilty of the cold-blooded and premeditated murder of the Honourable Ronald Adair, he would, in 1894, have gone to the gallows. Since he survived, it follows that he was found not guilty.

With Moran's acquittal he once more became a potential threat to Sherlock Holmes. But this time there was the threat of a further charge to hold over him. He had tried, in front of witnesses, to kill Holmes. If brought to court for that offence he would certainly face a lengthy term of imprisonment. Inspector Lestrade was keen to charge Moran, but Holmes, for two very good reasons, stuck to his original decision: "I do not propose to appear in the matter at all."

He knew that if Moran was accused of attempted murder against Sherlock Holmes, the court was likely to hear some rather embarrassing facts as a plea of mitigation. Sherlock Holmes did not want any further public discussion of the circumstances under which James Moriarty met his death. The Professor's brother had already made a number of allegations. Moran could have made many more, and the dock at the Old Bailey would have given him an ideal platform. From there his words would have reached the widest possible audience and he would have had the full protection of the law against any action for defamation.

Quite apart from his embarrassment at having Moran in the dock, Holmes was also unwilling to appear in court himself and this was for a reason connected with his future career. He wanted to get back to work as a detective. But the publicity campaign by Mycroft and Watson had been so successful that there was hardly a person in England, Europe or the United States who had not heard the name 'Sherlock Holmes'. If they had not read Watson's stories, they may well have seen the stage plays. After the Charles Rogers production in 1894, theatrical interest in Holmes

---

3) In 1914 Holmes referred to Moran in the present tense, thus implying he was still alive (*His Last Bow*).

as a character was growing and public interest bordered on adoration. Ironically, although this had been the means of protecting Holmes from any repercussions from the death of Moriarty, it now meant that if it became generally known he was still alive and had not perished at the Reichenbach Falls, he would have been fêted in such a way that he would have found it impossible to work. He would have been recognised and greeted everywhere he went. The world would have beaten a congratulatory path to the door of 221B Baker Street. He could never have acted as a detective under those conditions. And one certain way to announce to the world that Sherlock Holmes was still alive, was for him to appear in a major criminal court case. No record of any such case exists so we can be sure that Moran was never tried for the attempted murder of Sherlock Holmes.

Then what happened to him? Holmes, we know, was aware in 1902 that Moran was still alive. He had obviously ceased to be a threat and there can be little doubt that he had become a broken man after the events of 1894. Three years before, he had seen his old friend Moriarty murdered by Holmes. Then Holmes had killed Moran's young friend Adair and Moran himself had stood trial for the murder. The prospect of a long term of imprisonment for the attempted murder of Sherlock Holmes was too daunting a prospect for Colonel Moran and, after living under the shadow of the gallows for a period of weeks, he had no inclination to try to kill Holmes again. It was no doubt with some relief that Moran accepted Holmes's offer: go abroad, make a new life in South Africa and never again return to England.

CHAPTER TWELVE

The Official Agent

In the summer of 1894 the Moriarty affair was finally over and Sherlock Holmes was keen to get back to his career as a detective. He still had his Baker Street premises and his powers of observation and deduction, and there were no constraints upon him save one: as far as the world was concerned Sherlock Holmes had died at the Reichenbach Falls, locked in a struggle with Professor Moriarty.

The public is not in the habit of consulting the dead in matters of detection, so it was clear that Holmes must be resurrected. But, as we know, Watson did not publish his account of *The Empty House*, making clear that Sherlock Holmes had survived, until October, 1903, almost a decade later.

Would it not have been simpler for that account to have been published in 1894, making it possible for Holmes to immediately take up his practice again, without the ludicrous difficulty that most people believed him dead? The answer is 'no'. In the period of Holmes's absence from London, the publicity campaign consisting mainly of Watson's reports in the *Strand Magazine* had been so successful that Sherlock Holmes had become internationally famous. His adventures were read and re-read. Actors portrayed him on stage and it was to be only some six years later that he would be the central character in a silent film, entitled *Sherlock Holmes Baffled*. If the account of *The Empty House* had been published in 1894, it would have meant that Sherlock Holmes would have been fêted by an adoring public to such a degree that he would never again have been able to function as a detective.

It was a dilemma. Alive, Sherlock Holmes would be so well-known that he could not pursue his chosen career; dead, or apparently dead, he would be unable to get any clients.

And there was another complication: Holmes, for financial

reasons, needed to get back to work. Although he had been earning substantial sums of money immediately prior to his disappearance, he had not earned anything for the three years of his absence. In this period he had travelled the world and had kept up the Baker Street rooms for which, as Watson remarked in *The Dying Detective*, the payments had become 'princely'. There can be little doubt that the bank account of the once wealthy and successful Sherlock Holmes was severely depleted. Watson, ironically, was probably better off than Holmes at this point, since he had not only been running his medical practice, but had also had the benefit of the earnings from the stories about Holmes which he had published[1].

There was, perhaps, no urgency about Sherlock Holmes's situation, but nevertheless he would have wanted an early solution to his problem. The answer was provided by Mycroft: Sherlock Holmes could not operate if he was known to be alive; therefore, as far as the public was concerned, he must remain dead. As far as clients were concerned, Holmes would receive a substantial retainer from official sources (arranged by Mycroft) so that his services would be available to Scotland Yard and to the Government as an investigative agent. Eventually it was thought the euphoria over Watson's accounts of Holmes's adventures would die down, *The Empty House* could be quietly published and Holmes, then officially alive, could widen his practice to include more private cases.

Of course, the interest in Holmes was not to end, but equally, as we will see, the supply of private clients never actually dried up. Just as today quantities of mail addressed to Sherlock Holmes are received by the Abbey National Building Society, which stands on the site of 221B Baker Street, even then there were those people who were either unaware, or unwilling to accept, that Sherlock Holmes was dead. In time of trouble they became his clients.

The arrangement with the Government seems to have lasted until the end of 1898. In that period, Watson recorded thirteen cases of which six were either brought to Baker Street by police officers or the client was sent on by Scotland Yard. Two of the thirteen came to Holmes by chance, in that he was in the place

1) Watson and Doyle divided the royalties from the Sherlock Holmes stories.

where the mystery had occurred. In five of them Holmes was consulted directly by private clients. However, even in these five cases it is worth noting that one of the clients was referred to Holmes by a lawyer and another was himself a solicitor. It may well have been that the legal profession had been officially notified that Mr. Sherlock Holmes was alive and well and living in Baker Street. In that event, only three of the thirteen cases can be regarded as being where Holmes was consulted directly by a member of the public.

Watson also referred to twenty-one other cases in the same period. Of these, at least ten (and probably more) would have been official investigations. These would include the tracking and arrest of Huret the boulevard assassin, the investigation into the sudden death of Cardinal Tosca, the summons to Norway in 1895, the case of Victor Lynch, the case of Arthur Staunton, the case of Henry Staunton and four cases in which Holmes helped Inspector Stanley Hopkins, but which are not detailed by Watson.

It is clear from the records we have of Holmes's work in this period that the bulk of his cases were official.

In *The Golden Pince-Nez* in the November of 1894, Holmes was consulted by Inspector Stanley Hopkins. Hopkins again consulted him in July, 1895, in the affair of *Black Peter*. In November, 1895, Holmes acted for the British Government in the matter of the Bruce Partington submarine plans, while in *The Abbey Grange* in January, 1897, it was again Stanley Hopkins who called Holmes in. Hopkins had also sent Cyril Overton, who was concerned about the disappearance of a rugby player in *The Missing Threequarter*, along to Baker Street in the December of 1896, and in July, 1898, Josiah Amberley, a retired colourman, was sent by the Yard to consult Holmes over the disappearance of his wife.

Of his other cases, the client in *The Sussex Vampire*, in November, 1896, had been referred to Holmes by his lawyers and John Hector MacFarlane, who came to Holmes for help in August, 1895, over *The Norwood Builder*, was himself a solicitor.

Holmes was involved by chance in the *Adventure of the Three Students* in April, 1895. He and Watson were spending some weeks in 'one of our great university towns' when there was a problem over an examination paper. Holmes, since he was there, was asked to sort it all out. Similarly it was March, 1897, during a holiday in Cornwall that Holmes and Watson became involved in the Cornish horror, which Watson eventually called *The Devil's Foot*. Because of the element of chance, both of these cases are outside the normal pattern of Sherlock Holmes's business.

Of the remaining three cases we know that Mrs. Ronder, *The Veiled Lodger*, was referred to Holmes by her landlady who suggested: "There's this detective man what we read about." But what brought Violet Smith to Sherlock Holmes's door in April, 1895, in the affair of *The Solitary Cyclist*, or how Squire Hilton Cubitt came to consult the detective, we do not know. Perhaps, like Mrs. Ronder's landlady, they had heard of the detective, but were not aware that he was supposed to have died. Possibly they were referred to him, but Watson did not bother to record that fact. However, what is certain is that in this period Holmes was working almost continually for the authorities. Watson admitted as much in *The Solitary Cyclist*: "It is safe to say that there was no public case of any difficulty in which he was not consulted" between the years of 1894 and 1901. Watson added that there were also 'hundreds' of private cases during this period, but he did not furnish us with even the sketchiest details of most. Nevertheless, it is significant that he differentiated between 'public' and 'private' cases.

Holmes clearly had some sort of official standing. In December, 1896, in *The Missing Threequarter*, while trying to discover the contents of a telegram, he eyed the telegraph office and told Watson: "With a warrant we could demand to see the counterfoils." Really. A member of the police force, armed with a warrant, would have been able to, but a private individual would never have managed to get such a warrant. This is a clear indication of Holmes's official status. It cannot be dismissed as the mere wishful thinking of the unofficial agent, for Holmes added: "We have not reached that stage yet", clearly implying that when and if that stage was reached he would get a warrant.

Sherlock Holmes, after the uncertainties of the early 1890s, had regained his old pre-eminence as a detective. No longer were there the constant blunders, he had regained his old flair and competence and was handling cases of the highest importance, as well as rebuilding the private side of his practice.

Watson had become a full partner in the detective practice in 1894 when Holmes re-established himself in Baker Street. We know that it was at Holmes's request that Watson - whose wife had died shortly before - had sold his practice and returned to share 'the old quarters'[2]. Watson claimed that his practice was bought by a Dr. Verner, who had paid 'the best price that I ventured to ask'. This was fortunate for Watson, but he adds that some years later he discovered Verner was a distant relative of Holmes, and it was Holmes who 'had really found the money'.

Holmes would have been stretched to buy a medical practice in 1894. Much as he may have wanted Watson to return to Baker Street, the cost would have been too much for him. However, it would not have been impossible for him to have arranged a loan for Verner to buy the practice, the cash possibly coming from Mycroft.

In his account of *The Golden Pince-Nez* - the first case which Watson recorded after Holmes's reappearance - Watson referred to 'three massive manuscript volumes which contain our work for the year 1894' - the possessive pronoun showing clearly that the cases were no longer 'Sherlock Holmes's cases', they were then 'our work'. Watson had a proprietorial interest in the practice. His medical work was far behind him. As he remarked in *The Missing Threequarter*: "It argues the degree in which I had lost touch with my profession that the name of Leslie Armstrong was unknown to me. Now I am aware that he is not only one of the heads of the medical school of the University, but a thinker of European reputation in more than one branch of science." This was in December, 1896, and here was Watson not recognising the name of one of the most eminent medical men alive. But he was not practising medicine or even pretending to, he was now practising another profession - that of private detective.

2)   Mary Morstan died early in 1892. One researcher has ascribed her death to heart trouble inherited from her father. Twice in *The Sign of Four* she turned faint on very slight provocation (T.S. Blakeney. *Sherlock Holmes: Fact or Fiction*. London, 1932).

CHAPTER THIRTEEN

The Unscrupulous Accessory

Mycroft Holmes had entertained grave doubts over his brother's conduct in connection with the death of Professor Moriarty and he was, no doubt, happy that after 1894 Sherlock Holmes had become an arm of the official force where a degree of supervision covered his activities. There had, after all, been unfortunate rumours in the late 1880s over the lengths to which Sherlock Holmes was prepared to go to satisfy an influential client and earn a large fee.

With Watson, a man of irreproachable reputation, a partner in the firm, and the bulk of Holmes's cases and clients coming from the authorities, Mycroft probably felt that he had nothing more to fear from his younger brother. And for a while things went smoothly. In *The Golden Pince-Nez*, in November, 1894, Holmes successfully unravelled the murder of young Willoughby Smith, handing the murderess over to Inspector Hopkins. She cheated justice with a draft of poison, but that had been nothing that Holmes was able to prevent. In April the following year, Holmes had solved a case of examination cheating at a famous university and in the same month had saved Miss Violet Smith from being forced into marriage. This case, *The Solitary Cyclist*, had resulted in jail sentences of seven and ten years for the major villains. The *Black Peter* affair in July, 1895, again ended in a murderer being successfully brought to trial. That August, Holmes was successful in saving John Hector MacFarlane from being found guilty of a murder that never was. He produced the 'victim' alive for Inspector Lestrade and showed that the villain of the piece had been the supposed victim, a man who eventually went before a jury charged with conspiracy. In November, 1895,

Holmes was called in by Mycroft to investigate the death of a junior clerk at Woolwich Arsenal and the disappearance of the Bruce Partington submarine plans. It was a highly successful case.

Mycroft must have been gratified at his brother's new-found stability. In October, 1896, Holmes was brought into the case of *The Veiled Lodger* by a Brixton landlady. The lodger in question, Mrs. Ronder, merely wanted to relate her terrible story to a 'man of judgement', but even so Holmes was able to help her. "Your life is not your own," he told her. "Keep your hands off it." His entreaty was successful and she sent to 221B the bottle of prussic acid with which she had intended to end her life. The case of *The Sussex Vampire*, in November, 1896, was again a success for Holmes. He was able to free Mr. Robert Ferguson of the suspicion that his Peruvian-born wife was in the habit of biting her baby son's neck and sucking his blood. In December that year Sherlock Holmes discovered the whereabouts of *The Missing Threequarter* and the tragic circumstances which had caused him to miss the Oxford-Cambridge rugby match, again a successful and competently handled investigation. Watson, as Holmes's medical adviser, and now his partner, must have shared Mycroft's satisfaction at the way things were going.

On Saturday, 23rd January, 1897, a note from Stanley Hopkins arrived at Baker Street. It was the beginning of the case of *The Abbey Grange* and the events were to sound a warning bell in Watson's mind that all, perhaps, was not as it should be. In his note, Hopkins, writing from Marsham, Kent, asked for Holmes's assistance 'in what promises to be a most remarkable case'. It was, he told Holmes, 'something quite in your line'.

What was this 'most remarkable case'? Sir Eustace Brackenstall, 'one of the richest men in Kent', had been found dead in his own home, his head 'knocked in with a poker'. The window was open and there had been a robbery. Hardly very mysterious. In fact it all seems very straightforward. A burglary and a brutal murder. Surely this was not something in Sherlock Holmes's 'line'.

Hopkins had written his note at 3.30 a.m. Lady Brackenstall at that time had not been able to explain what had happened, but before Holmes and Watson arrived she had given Hopkins 'so clear an account of the affair there is not much left for us to do'.

What Lady Brackenstall had done, in fact, was just confirm that the murder followed a robbery. She had also described the robbers and Hopkins thought the men responsible were a gang from Lewisham, the three Randalls, a father and two sons.

The question is: why is this case so remarkable and something in Holmes's line when Hopkins writes his notes, yet a few hours later, when those self-same facts are confirmed, Hopkins tells Holmes: "I should not have troubled you."

Sherlock Holmes, after all, is not the kind of investigator who would get much satisfaction from looking into this kind of crime - on the face of it there was absolutely no mystery.

The words 'something quite in your line' must mean that some aspect of the case would interest Holmes. What could that be? There's no mystery about the crime, possibly something about the people.

Significantly Sir Eustace was very rich; his widow now is presumably also very rich. Could it be that this is what was in Holmes's 'line'? Very rich people were involved and, at a time like this, would be very vulnerable. There can be no other conclusion. Hopkins called Holmes in because of the amount of money in the case. While the killers were still unknown there was a chance something could be made out of it, but once Lady Brackenstall had given her description the affair was as good as over and there was nothing that Holmes could do.

Indeed, before Hopkins gave him the bad news, Sherlock Holmes was very conscious of the financial aspects of the case. On the way to Marsham he told Watson: "We are moving in the high life." There is a gleeful, almost handrubbing tone to the comment. Watson probably left a word out of this remark by Holmes when he set it down. Holmes most likely said: "We are moving in the high life again."

Cases involving the rich had been thin on the ground for Holmes since he had returned in 1894. Watson left us no detailed cases in which Holmes moved in the upper strata of society between 1894 and *The Abbey Grange*. True, he mentions in passing the death of Cardinal Tosca in 1895 and the problem which Holmes investigated for the tobacco millionaire, John Vincent Harding, and we may surmise that these involved high level inquiries, but this is only supposition. *The Abbey Grange* is the first hard evidence we have of Holmes regaining his position as a detective consulted by high society, although in this instance, of course, it is Hopkins who brought him in.

As it all turned out, there was no robbery. A former lover of Lady Brackenstall called Croker (he knew her before her marriage) had turned up, found that Sir Eustace mistreated his wife and hit him over the head with the poker. Lady Brackenstall and Croker then set to work to cover up what had really happened and make the whole thing look like a robbery.

Holmes eventually discovered the truth, yet he took no action to bring the guilty to book. Instead, he allowed the police to continue with their search for the gang they thought responsible for the crime. He took a rather lenient view of the whole thing. He told Lady Brackenstall that he wanted her to treat him 'as a friend'. "You may find that I will justify your trust," he said, adding, "I will not cause you any unnecessary trouble ... my whole desire is to make things easier for you."

And, even more amazingly, when he taxed Croker on the subject he told him flatly: "You are acquitted."

Croker was free to return after a respectable period and marry Lady Brackenstall, one of the richest women in Kent.

This is hardly the new, stable, law-abiding Sherlock Holmes. This is the Holmes of the 1880s, freely allowing a killer and his accomplice to go free. And, incidentally, making himself and Dr. Watson accessories in the crime, which could have been found to be murder, though most likely it would have been manslaughter.

There was no moral justification for Holmes's behaviour. Sir

Eustace may have been a drunkard who mistreated his wife, but that did not make his death justifiable. Lady Brackenstall could, after all, have left him. Yet Holmes allowed Croker and the lady not merely to be free of the entanglement of the unpleasant Sir Eustace, but also to profit handsomely by his death.

Holmes, of course, kept conclusive proof of what had really happened. He told Croker that 'as long as the law does not find some other victim' he would take no further action. The Randalls had by this time been arrested in New York for something else and therefore could not have had a hand in the crime.

Croker and Lady Brackenstall were free to profit from the death of Sir Eustace and Sherlock Holmes held a secret that they would have both paid a great deal not to have revealed.

Dr. Watson seems to have been carried along with Holmes's eagerness to take no action against the pair. As he admitted, when Holmes appointed him the 'jury' to decide on Croker's guilt or innocence, Watson replied 'not guilty'. However, a couple of months later, we learn that Holmes's constitution 'showed symptoms of giving way in the pace of constant hard work of a most exacting kind, aggravated, perhaps, by occasional indiscretions of his own'. Watson tells us that Dr Moore Agar of Harley Street had given 'positive injunctions' that Holmes should lay aside all his cases and surrender himself to complete rest 'if he wished to avert an absolute breakdown'.

Holmes was 'induced at last, on the threat of being permanently disqualified from work, to give himself a complete change of scene and air'.

This is surely more than coincidence. Sherlock Holmes apparently lapsed into his old ways, making himself an accessory to crime, letting a killer go free and keeping the criminal in his power by retaining proof of the crime, and the next thing we hear is that he was ordered to stop work and rest. If he refused he was threatened 'with permanent disqualification' from his work. Watson, no doubt, thought the Abbey Grange affair over and realised the implications of Holmes's actions. He would have

Occasionally he *was* the Government. Mycroft Holmes in 1900.

discussed his fears with Mycroft, who would have seen that the result could well be scandal. Quite apart from letting the killer go free and his illegal actions in the crime itself, Mycroft would have been disquieted by the odd terms in which the note from Stanley Hopkins was couched. It smelled of corruption. Here was a young detective calling in Holmes in a situation where Holmes's only interest could have been money. Mycroft would have found that Hopkins had been involved with Holmes in six recent cases before the Abbey Grange affair and, no doubt, would have been concerned about the relationship between the two, a relationship which, The Abbey Grange showed, was highly suspect.

To prevent a scandal, Mycroft would have acted immediately. Hopkins would have been transferred to duties taking him out of temptation's way, and indeed he is never again mentioned in Watson's writings. What to do about Sherlock Holmes was a different matter. In the end, Mycroft arranged a meeting between Sherlock and the Harley Street consultant, Dr. Moore Agar, who was briefed to instruct Holmes that he needed a complete rest. True, Holmes had been working hard, but it was the 'occasional indiscretions' that were the real reason for the rest. Holmes clearly brushed aside the pleas that he should temporarily cease work for the sake of his health, but was eventually persuaded to take a holiday.

To the casual reader it may be thought that Watson implied Holmes was 'induced' to rest by Dr. Moore Agar. But in fact Watson was careful not to say that. He deliberately linked the consultant's health warning with the threat. But he did not attribute the threat to anybody. If it had been Moore Agar, Watson would have said so, but because he left it deliberately vague, it becomes clear that someone else made the threat. That someone was Mycroft. He would have revealed to Sherlock that he was aware of his 'indiscretion' in the Abbey Grange case (and other indiscretions possibly) and told Sherlock that unless he took an immediate rest, staying away until Dr. Watson was satisfied he was recovered, he would have to cease his practice. Mycroft

Holmes, as next of kin, Dr. Watson and Dr. Moore Agar, together could, in the final event, have had Holmes committed to a mental institution for a period[1]. Reluctantly, Sherlock Holmes would have accepted his brother's instructions, leaving London for Cornwall. It was a holiday that kept Holmes out of active practice for over a year. He and Watson left at the end of February or early in March, 1897, and he did not resume his practice in London until 27th July the following year.

Soon after their arrival in Cornwall, Holmes and Watson were involved in the horror of *The Devil's Foot*. The vicar of the hamlet of Tredannick Wollas and Mr. Mortimer Tregennis, who lodged in the vicarage, called upon Holmes and Watson in the small white-washed cottage they had taken near Poldhu Bay. A tragedy had occurred during the night and the vicar thought it must be a 'special Providence' that Holmes was in the neighbourhood. Mr. Mortimer Tregennis had spent the previous evening playing cards with his two brothers and their sister Brenda at their house of Tredannick Wartha. When he left them all was well, but the following morning they were discovered still sitting round the card table, Brenda stone-dead and the two brothers shouting and singing 'the senses stricken clean out of them'. Later, Mr. Mortimer Tregennis was to die of the same symptoms. The cause of the deaths was a little known West African poison which when heated or placed on a fire gave off toxic fumes. Mortimer Tregennis had used the substance on his sister and two brothers for the sake of money. Brenda's lover, Leon Sterndale, had dashed to the village and used the same poison on Mortimer Tregennis. Holmes successfully unravelled the case, but he refused to take any action against Sterndale. Again Holmes made himself an accessory to a serious crime. True, Watson recorded that Sherlock Holmes said to him: "You would not denounce the man?" and Watson claimed to have

---

1) Under British law at the time it required two doctors to certify a person insane and have him committed. The fact that Moore Agar was called in to reinforce Watson demonstrates that Mycroft was prepared, if necessary, to take this step.

replied "certainly not". Whether that exchange actually occurred or whether, when he came to write up the story later, Watson was simply being loyal to his friend, we do not know. But since Holmes was in Cornwall almost as a direct result of a similar action, Watson would have been aware that he was not yet ready to return to Baker Street and the caseload which awaited him.

The Devil's Foot took place in March, 1897. Watson did not allow Holmes to return to London for twelve months. At the end of that period, Watson judged his friend ready to go back into practice and it was in July of 1898 that Holmes became involved in the affair of *The Dancing Men*. To Watson's and, no doubt, Mycroft's relief, Holmes acted quite properly throughout the inquiry and, although his client, Mr. Hilton Cubitt of Ridlingthorpe Manor, Norfolk, was shot dead by his wife's former lover before the affair ended, Holmes could not be blamed in any way. He handed over the murderer to the police and his conduct was above reproach. So too was it the same month when he investigated the disappearance of the wife of Josiah Amberley, *The Retired Colourman*. Mr. Ray Ernest, who lived nearby, had disappeared at the same time and Holmes established that the pair had been locked in Amberley's strongroom and gas pumped in. Amberley was handed over to the police by Holmes, who did not want to take any credit for the case.

It is noticeable at this time that Holmes was taking things a lot easier. After the Abbey Grange case in January, 1897, it was, if we ignore his chance involvement in *The Devil's Foot*, some eighteen months before he had another case, *The Dancing Men*. *The Retired Colourman* case took place at about the same time, as did the case of the two Coptic Patriarchs. But after this brief period of activity, it was to be almost seven months before Holmes had his next case - that of Charles Augustus Milverton.

The reason for Holmes's apparent lack of activity may well have been that Watson and Mycroft thought it advisable that he did not become overloaded with work. They did not want any repetition of his illegal behaviour. But the Milverton case was to see yet more, and this time overwork could not be the cause. Milverton was a notorious blackmailer and Holmes had been employed to recover some incriminating letters written by Lady Eva Brackwell, who was to be married a fortnight later to the Earl of Dovercourt. Milverton was threatening to send the letters - 'imprudent, nothing worse' - to the Earl, unless a large sum of money was paid to him. Holmes told Watson that the letters would 'suffice to break off the match'.

An attempt to buy the letters back failed and Holmes resolved to take direct action. "I mean to burgle Milverton's house tonight," he told Watson.

The doctor was aghast. "For heaven's sake, Holmes, think what you are doing," he cried.

Holmes said that his plan, although 'technically criminal', was 'morally justifiable'. Watson turned it over in his mind and agreed 'so long as our object is to take no articles save those which are used for an illegal purpose'.

On balance, Watson's view may well be right. To steal the instrument of blackmail from a blackmailer and destroy it can hardly be reprehensible. Watson's anguished cry of 'think what you are doing' may well have been prompted by the warnings that Holmes had received from his brother that if he was involved in any more law-breaking, Mycroft would take steps to see that he did not practice again.

As things turned out it may well have been all too much for Watson. The break-in was successful, but as they were rummaging through the contents of Milverton's safe. The blackmailer returned. Holmes and Watson took refuge behind a curtain and were surprised to hear an interview going on in the room between Milverton and one of his female victims. The woman claimed that Milverton had ruined her marriage and emptied a revolver into him. Fortunately none of the shots went anywhere near the curtain that concealed Holmes and Watson. They did, however, manage to get a glimpse of the lady doing the shooting. After she had gone, Holmes quickly locked the door and burned the letters which were concealed in Milverton's safe. The letter by which the woman with the revolver had gained access to Milverton - 'the messenger of death' - still lay on Milverton's desk, 'all mottled with his blood'. Holmes added it to the fire. Then, with the sound of people hammering on the locked door, Holmes and Watson made their escape through the window, scaled a six foot garden wall (Watson was forced to kick off a pursuer who grabbed at his ankle), and finally ran two miles across Hampstead Heath to make good their getaway.

What Watson thought of the whole affair we can only guess. But while it was one thing to carry out, from the best of motives, the burglary, covering up the murder of Milverton was another. And this was not simply a case of Holmes refusing to take any action which would help the police bring the killer to justice. He had actually burned the letter which had been the pretext for the fatal interview. Not only that, he and Watson had been chased from the scene of the crime. If they had been identified, they could well have found themselves under suspicion of carrying out the killing themselves.

Doubtless Watson felt something of a shiver down his spine the morning after the murder of Milverton, when Inspector Lestrade called just after breakfast time. What was worse, he had called in connection with the Milverton affair, and his suspects, seen at Milverton's house, were two men 'as nearly as possible captured red-handed'. Lestrade was fairly confident that he would be able to trace the pair. "We have their footmarks, we have their description," he told Holmes.

Watson probably did not find it very amusing when, after the Inspector had given a description of one of the suspects, Holmes remarked: "Why it might be a description of Watson!" And Lestrade's amused agreement would not have helped Watson digest his breakfast that morning.

Holmes, however, decided against getting involved in the police investigation, probably to Watson's relief. Lunchtime found Holmes and Watson standing outside a shop in Oxford

Street with a window filled with photographs of the celebrities and beauties of the day. One of the pictures was of 'a regal and stately lady in Court dress, with a high diamond tiara upon her noble head'. Watson, recognising her as the woman with the revolver, caught his breath as he read the 'time-honoured title of the great nobleman and statesman whose wife she had been'.

Knowing the identity of the killer would not have made Watson's conscience any easier. It would, if anything, have added to his burden. He now knew the identity of the murderer of Milverton; he had been an eye-witness to the crime (while committing a crime himself, incidentally); and he had seen Sherlock Holmes destroy material evidence. On top of all that, he was being hunted by the police, suspected of the crime. Holmes had, without doubt, put him in an impossible position.

There is little doubt that it was about this time that Watson began examining his conscience with regard to the behaviour of Sherlock Holmes. All of the last five cases, that is, *The Abbey Grange*, *The Devil's Foot*, *The Dancing Men*, *The Retired Colourman* and *Charles Augustus Milverton*, had involved murder. In each case Holmes had discovered the killer, yet in only two of those cases had he turned the murderer over to the police. In the other three, he had decided that the guilty should go free, and by doing so had involved himself and Watson directly in the crime.

It was a difficult situation for Dr. Watson, and one that was not resolved when Holmes became involved, at the request of Inspector Lestrade, in the case of *The Six Napoleons* in June, 1900. This concerned the mysterious series of thefts of plaster busts of the Emperor Napoleon. In each case the bust was almost immediately smashed by the thief. Holmes discovered that the 'famous black pearl of the Borgias', stolen at the time the plaster busts were made, had been concealed inside one of the busts and that the thief was trying to find it. Five of the six busts had been destroyed and Holmes learned that the sixth was owned by a Mr. Sandeford of Reading. Mr. Sandeford had bought it for fifteen shillings, and felt compelled to admit as much when Holmes offered him ten pounds for it. Sandeford, who did not know what the bust contained, was willing to sell and at Holmes's request signed a paper transferring 'every possible right' he might have had in the bust to Sherlock Holmes.

When he had gone, Holmes broke the bust open and revealed the 'enormously valuable' pearl.

Despite the thoroughness of Holmes's investigation, the equal thoroughness with which Holmes legally acquired the last remaining bust gives pause for thought. The patently honest Mr. Sandeford was sent away with his ten pound note while Sherlock Holmes remained with the pearl. True, it would have had to go back to its owner, but no doubt the reward, on a percentage basis, would have been substantial. Did not Sandeford deserve better?

Watson next recorded Holmes in action 'after a month of trivialities and stagnation' in Thor Bridge, which took place in October, 1900. Here Sherlock Holmes was retained by Mr. J. Neil Gibson, a millionaire gold king from America and then the owner of Thor Place, a large estate in Hampshire. Gibson's Brazilian-born wife had been found late at night on Thor Bridge, in the grounds of the house, in dinner dress and shawl with a revolver bullet through her brain. A revolver of similar calibre and with one chamber fired was found in the wardrobe of Miss Grace Dunbar, the governess for the two Gibson children. The evidence against Miss Dunbar, who had seemed for some time to be the likeliest successor to Mrs. Gibson in the event of her death, was strong. The dead woman had a note upon her making an appointment with the governess at the place of the tragedy and Miss Dunbar was seen in the vicinity of the bridge at the time. Holmes had few problems with the case. Although in the end he castigated himself as 'sluggish' for not having seen the solution earlier, he eventually cleared Miss Dunbar by demonstrating that Mrs. Gibson, who was jealous of her, committed suicide in such a way as to make it appear the governess had murdered her. Perhaps after this well-handled investigation Watson once more thought Holmes was abandoning his old ways.

If he did, he was wrong. Sherlock Holmes was to be seen at his very worst in May of the following year. Watson mentioned only a couple of cases in the intervening months, so it is likely that with few official investigations coming in - Mycroft having put a stop to them - and with the public in general still thinking Holmes was dead, that cases were a little thin on the ground. Cash too, perhaps, for it was money that was Holmes's first concern when Mr. Thorneycroft Huxtable called at Baker Street on Thursday, 16th May, 1901.

Mr. Huxtable was a rather scruffy schoolmaster, who called on Holmes because he wanted the detective to 'come to Mackleton (in northern England) with me by the next train'. But the unprepossessing appearance of the man did not interest Holmes. He shook his head at the request. "We are very busy at present," he declared royally.

Huxtable, however, was eventually able to gain Holmes's interest. He mentioned the name 'Duke of Holdernesse' and said that the Duke's son had been abducted. Holmes' arm immediately shot across to pick up the reference encyclopædia where he checked the Duke's entry. He already knew Holdernesse was a former Cabinet Minister, but the book told him in addition that the Duke 'owns about two hundred and fifty thousand acres' as well as mineral rights, a castle in Wales, a hall in Hallamshire and a fashionable London address.

Holmes was impressed. "Well, well, this man is certainly one of the greatest subjects of the Crown", he remarked.

Huxtable added that the Duke was 'perhaps the wealthiest' and went on to tell Holmes there was a reward of five thousand pounds for the return of the Duke's son and a further one thousand for naming the kidnapper or kidnappers.

Money talks and Holmes was convinced. The cases which would have kept him too busy to work for a humble schoolmaster were forgotten. "Watson, I think we shall accompany Mr. Huxtable back to the North of England."

The result of the matter was that Holmes eventually learnt that the Duke's son and heir, Lord Saltire, had been kidnapped by the Duke's illegitimate son James Wilder, who was in league with a local innkeeper. During the course of the abduction, the innkeeper had killed a schoolmaster who went to Lord Saltire's assistance.

But when Holmes eventually learnt the truth, he decided that the best thing to do was to allow the innkeeper, Reuben Hayes, who had already been arrested, to take all the blame for the affair and go to the gallows.

The architect of the plot, James Wilder, was to go scot free, packed off to Australia. If this seems a little unfair on Hayes, we must remember that Holmes was working for the Duke who, apart from getting his son back, wanted to 'minimize this hideous scandal'. Holmes, who may have earned twelve thousand pounds from the case, said that he was 'disposed to help' to the best of his ability.

It is, of course, entirely possible that had Wilder gone into the dock alongside Hayes, both would have hanged. It is just as likely that as Wilder was the ringleader, he would have gone to the gallows while his accomplice would have faced a lesser punishment. That was of no concern to Sherlock Holmes. It was of no interest at all whether an innkeeper hanged or was sentenced to life imprisonment. Most important was keeping Wilder out of it.

Holmes advised the Duke that Hayes must not be allowed to divulge the truth in court. "I have no doubt your Grace could make him understand it is in his interest to remain silent." This was a hint that the Duke should promise a substantial sum of money to Hayes's dependants in the event he remained silent.

As far as the police are concerned, Hayes 'kidnapped the boy for the purpose of ransom,' said Holmes, who was not going to let them into the secret. "If they do not themselves find it out, I see no reason why I should prompt them." One reason, of course, might be a desire to see justice done. But the size of the fee had overcome any of Holmes's scruples.

Holmes tried to give the impression that while he knew the truth, there was no reason for him to tell the police what had really happened. However, what he was doing went far beyond that. He was advising the Duke to silence Hayes. He was happily seeing Wilder - the real villain and a man with nothing to recommend him, save he was the Duke's son - being given a new start overseas, and he had valuable evidence about the kidnapping and murder which he chose to suppress. Holmes was actively engaged with the Duke, with Wilder, in staging a cover-up. If the police had discovered what really went on at Mackleton and the parts played by Sherlock Holmes and the Duke of Holdernesse, there can be little doubt that Holmes would have found himself in the dock facing a charge of conspiring with others to pervert the course of justice.

How much Holmes was paid for these services is not entirely clear, and has been much discussed by other writers. The fee being offered originally was six thousand pounds. However, after Holmes uncovered some incriminating evidence, the Duke offered to double that to twelve thousand to ensure Holmes's discretion. Holmes said: "I fear, your Grace, that matters can hardly be arranged so easily." He was unlikely to be hinting that twelve thousand pounds would be insufficient: it was a fortune; but neither was he refusing to accept it. He was simply making it clear to the Duke that there were things to do before the question of payment came into it. Writing a cheque would not halt events. Holmes would not have felt any compunction about taking the larger figure from the Duke, a man who could clearly afford it.

Watson never recorded his feelings about the whole unpleasant affair, but he was soon to take decisive action, demonstrating his disapproval at the way things had turned out in Baker Street.

CHAPTER FOURTEEN

The Final Moves

By July, 1902, Dr. Watson was feeling 'rheumatic and old'. He was approaching his fiftieth birthday and was suffering from a painful leg wound which he had received the previous month in the affair of *The Three Garridebs*. He had narrowly escaped more serious injury when a confrontation with a criminal had developed into a gunfight and a shot had caught Watson in the thigh. The wound enforced a period of inactivity and, as his birthday neared, gave Watson the chance to review his life and achievements.

He had enjoyed considerable success as an author. His partnership with Arthur Conan Doyle in the early 1890s had given him a measure of financial security and they had repeated their success the previous year, 1901, with *The Hound of the Baskervilles*. As well as that, he was a partner in England's most prestigious private detective agency and the friend and associate of Sherlock Holmes, one of the most famous men in England.

But John Watson was not a happy man. He had started his career as a physician, but apart from his army service, had practised for only a little over five years in all, and had now totally lost touch with his old profession. He had been married twice, but each time widowed. The first Mrs. Watson had survived only a little over twelve months. His second marriage, to Mary Morstan, who he had met in *The Sign of Four*, had taken place in May, 1889. But less than three years later Mary was dead of a heart attack. He had no family[1] and, as he waited for his wound to heal, he realised that his whole life now revolved around Sherlock

---

1) Watson remarked in *A Study in Scarlet* that he had that he had 'neither kith nor kin' in England. This allows the possibility that he had family elsewhere in the world. However, he makes clear that his father was dead, as was his elder bother. Since he mentioned no other family it is safe to assume he had none.

Holmes's practice as a detective[2]. Even his stories were centred on Holmes and the cases they investigated together.

Watson felt he was in a rut. As he remarked about Holmes in *The Creeping Man*: "The relations between us in those latter days were peculiar. He was a man of habits, narrow and concentrated habits, and I had become one of them."

Watson was becoming somewhat disillusioned with Sherlock Holmes. The doctor was an honourable and straightforward man. The way Holmes had started to behave in recent years did not conform to the standard of ethical behaviour that he expected. one did not allow murderers to go free, carry out burglaries, or get involved in plots designed to pervert the course of justice. And one certainly did not get involved in such plots in return for money. Watson knew what was going on, and, as a partner in the practice, he was profiting from it. It was not a situation he liked, but he saw that as long as he was with Holmes, he would continue to be drawn into such affairs.

Only the previous May he had had the humiliating experience of being caught with Holmes in the act of breaking into a vault on the Shoscombe Old Place estate. There had followed the shooting in *The Three Garridebs*. Watson was, no doubt, delighted when, following his period of recuperation, Holmes suggested that he should take a trip to Lausanne to see if he could trace the missing Lady Frances Carfax.

In the course of the investigation, Watson was the victim of a murderous attack and, before Lady Frances was found, he saw Holmes again blundering onto private property without a warrant. On one occasion the police were called and Watson suffered the embarrassment of being escorted off the premises, in company with Holmes, by a uniformed police officer. Lady Frances was eventually traced and by that time Watson had reached a decision. He had had enough. He no longer wanted to be beaten up by

---

2) The doctor may also have wanted freedom to pursue an affair of the heart. He was married for the third time the following month, October, 1902.

thugs and he no longer wanted to he a party to Sherlock Holmes's illegal activities. He resolved to give up his share in the partnership, leave Baker Street and find rooms elsewhere.

He planned to keep in touch with Holmes and, perhaps, join him in the occasional case, but he wanted to be free of the day to day involvement. Watson did not go far. By the September of 1902 he had found himself an apartment in Queen Anne Street, not a stone's throw from Baker Street.

The pair still saw each other frequently. Watson had developed a taste for Turkish baths and he and Holmes would meet at an establishment in Northumberland Avenue.

In that September, Watson was at the baths when Holmes showed him the message from Sir James Damery which eventually led to the case of *The Illustrious Client*. Watson made sure he was at Baker Street to hear Sir James set out the matter; a certain illustrious person was at pains to prevent the marriage of Miss Violet de Merville, the daughter of General de Merville, to Baron Gruner, the Austrian murderer. Holmes, after being the subject of a murderous attack, used Watson to distract the evil Baron, while he burgled the house. His object was the Baron's 'lust diary' which he was to use to persuade the self-willed Miss de Merville that the marriage was not a good idea. In the course of things the Baron was attacked by a Miss Kitty Winter, who threw vitriol in his face, severely disfiguring him despite Watson's immediate ministrations. The lady eventually received the lowest possible sentence for the crime because of extenuating circumstances and Sherlock Holmes, 'although threatened with a prosecution for burglary', was never to stand in the dock.

As Watson remarked: "When an object is good and a client sufficiently illustrious, even the rigid British law becomes human and elastic". Nevertheless, Holmes had yet again become involved in illicit goings-on and had done little to restore Watson's faith in him. The same month, Inspector Gregson was a little perplexed at Holmes's involvement in *The Red Circle*, an affair of Italian secret societies. Holmes explained: "Education, Gregson, education. Still seeking knowledge at the old university." Gregson, it seems, was aware that Holmes's connection with official cases had ceased by this time.

In January, 1903, Sherlock Holmes was involved in the case of *The Blanched Soldier*. This was curious in that for the first time Holmes himself wrote the narrative. He was at pains to explain that he had taken up the pen because Watson had worried him for a long time to write an experience of his own.

Holmes, in his account, accused Watson of taking 'the only selfish action which I can recall in our association'.

Watson's crime? According to Holmes he 'had at that time deserted me for a wife ... I was alone'.

Watson had left Baker Street twice before when he took a wife. If he had married again, and if Holmes regarded that as a selfish act, it could hardly have been Watson's only selfish action. It would have been his third[3].

Surely Holmes had not forgotten the doctor's two previous marriages? Of course not, but he had to have a way to explain Watson's absence. He did not want to admit that Watson had left Baker Street because he did not like the way Holmes was going on. Holmes had always justified his illegal acts as being necessary or in a good cause. He refused to accept Watson's disapproval.

At this time, Holmes's career was in a decline and he needed Watson around to help him. In *The Blanched Soldier*, he described Watson as 'the ideal helpmate'. Holmes certainly felt that Watson had taken a selfish action, but the action he was referring to was leaving Baker Street, not for any good reason in Holmes's view (and taking a wife may have qualified as good reason), but rather for no reason. Holmes would not accept that Watson just wanted to get away. He needed the doctor around. By leaving, Watson was being selfish.

After *The Blanched Soldier*, Sherlock Holmes's career was

3) The identity of the third Mrs Watson has never been satisfactorily resolved. She has variously been identified as Lady Frances Carfax and Miss Violet de Merville, but there is no clear evidence for either.

nearing its end. From an impoverished student he had reached the heights of fame and wealth as a confidant to the mighty, but his breakdown and the murders of James Moriarty and Ronald Adair had ruined that, forcing him to return to London in the guise of a dead man. His ambition, however, had burned no less brightly, and the lengths to which he would go to satisfy a rich client and gain a substantial reward had worried Watson and horrified Mycroft. Official cases had eventually been withdrawn and in the end even Watson had felt there was no point in going on. He had left Baker Street for the last time, although the habit of half a lifetime died hard and he still kept in touch with Holmes.

On 26th May, 1903, Watson, on a visit to Baker Street, was alarmed by the intrusion of the negro bruiser, Steve Dixie, whose mission was to threaten Holmes and warn him off getting involved in the case of *The Three Gables*. By chance, therefore, Watson became involved in what was perhaps Holmes's most significant case - which certainly put an end to his career.

Holmes was acting for Mrs. Mary Maberley, who complained of 'a succession of strange incidents' at her home, including someone who offered to buy the premises, providing that everything inside the house was included.

Holmes discovered that a notorious adventuress, Isadora Klein, 'the celebrated beauty, the richest as well as the loveliest widow on earth', had been trying to get hold of the manuscript of a book from the house and had been responsible for a burglary in an effort to obtain it. The book, written by Mrs. Maberley's son, then dead, was based on an affair he had with Mrs. Klein and since all the characters could be identified, would ruin her reputation. "I wanted to do the thing honestly," she pleaded "I was ready to buy the house and everything in it. I offered any price she cared to ask. I only tried the other way when everything else failed - what else could I do with my whole future at stake?"

She could, of course, have consulted Sherlock Holmes. In *A Scandal in Bohemia* he was happily advising the King of Bohemia, first to buy back compromising documents, then to steal

Mrs Mary Maberley. Her case was the direct cause of the end of the career of Sherlock Holmes.

them. And it was Holmes who tricked his way into Irene Adler's house to try and get the papers back.

But Mrs. Klein had not taken the simple precaution of a visit to Baker Street. Instead, by taking action herself, she had placed herself in Holmes's hands. He would, naturally, keep quiet about the burglary at Three Gables which the police are looking into. "Well, well, I suppose I shall have to compound a felony as usual." But there is a price to be paid. "How much does it cost to go round the world in first class style?"

Holmes took a cheque for five thousand pounds for this supposed round-the-world trip from Isadora Klein. He assured her: "I will see it comes to Mrs. Maberley." But he was nevertheless careful to have it made out to himself. "Sign me a cheque," he told Mrs. Klein.

But if we stop to think, how could Sherlock Holmes go back to Mrs. Maberley, his client, and hand her a cheque for five thousand pounds with no explanation? She, after all, had engaged him to explain the strange happenings at her home. If he returned with no explanation - and by taking the cheque from Mrs. Klein he was bound to silence - but a gift of five thousand pounds. Mrs. Maberley was going to ask some questions.

She would want to know where the money came from. She was not the type of woman simply to sit back and accept whatever glib explanation Holmes could come up with. Even if Holmes told her the whole truth and swore her to secrecy, there was the risk that she might not want the money, but instead demand justice. Sherlock Holmes meanwhile had engaged in the blackmail of a woman desperate to protect her reputation from scandal, an activity the courts might well view seriously. He could not afford to have it come out that he agreed to keep silent about Mrs. Klein's affairs in exchange for money. And if he had tried to hand the money over to Mrs. Maberley, he would have been taking a vast risk.

Once he had the cheque, there was only one realistic course of action. He had to give Mrs. Maberley some sort of comforting explanation so that she would consider the matter closed, pay the Klein cheque into his own bank account and leave it there.

This case was in May, 1903. Five months later, as he was approaching his fiftieth birthday, Sherlock Holmes suddenly and with no warning announced his retirement. He left London and set up home at a lonely villa on the southern slope of the Sussex Downs. Watson was to pass 'almost beyond my ken' and an occasional visit was all that Holmes would see of him. There was no doubt that after his retirement Holmes missed the old life. In *The Lion's Mane* he admitted as much: "My house is lonely. I, my old housekeeper and my bees have the estate all to ourselves."

Exchanging his busy life in London for a quiet country retreat was hardly characteristic of Sherlock Holmes. After all, in *The Norwood Builder* in 1902 he had claimed his work was 'its own reward' and in only 1902 in *The Red Circle* he had said, 'it's art for art's sake, Watson'.

But suddenly, now, he was giving it all up. Why?

The answer lies in the Three Gables affair. The only recorded adventures of Holmes after *The Three Gables* and before his retirement are *The Mazarin Stone*, which occurred in the summer of 1903, and *The Creeping Man* in September of that year. Neither throws much light on Holmes's fate. *The Mazarin Stone* is of doubtful authorship, and although Dr. Watson makes an appearance in it. He was not the narrator and the affair was recounted by a third person. With its frequent references to airguns and wax dummies personifying Holmes, it may well be the product of someone's imagination. *The Creeping Man* was Watson's account of a visit to 'Camford' to discover the horrifying secret of Professor Presbury, who had been experimenting with monkey glands. Again it tells us little, save that Holmes and Watson's relationship had by this time, in Watson's words, become 'peculiar'.

The retirement was not due to anything detailed in either of those cases. It was almost certainly as a direct result of *The Three Gables* that Sherlock Holmes was forced to leave his practice and

London. He had blackmailed Mrs Klein for five thousand pounds, but had not taken the precaution of accepting the money in cash. He had taken a cheque, made out to himself. Consequently it was easy to establish that he had received the money.

Although he claimed he was going to hand it over to Mrs. Maberley, it was not a risk that he was able to take. If he had given it to her, it was more than likely that it would have been discovered where the money came from, and Holmes had obtained that money - no matter how he dressed it up - by an act of plain, old-fashioned blackmail.

But, as it turned out, hanging on to the money was just as dangerous. Mrs. Klein was, perhaps, not unhappy to part with the five thousand while she imagined it was going to take Mrs. Maberley on a world cruise. Mrs Klein had, after all, been very fond of Mrs. Maberley's dead son. But it would have been easy for her to establish that Mrs, Maberley did not go on the cruise, that she stayed home and, in fact, Sherlock Holmes kept the money. Mrs. Klein would have been angry at being blackmailed and Mrs. Maberley would have been angry at having been duped by the man she had hired - and she had probably handed over a fee as well - to sort out the mystery for her. Two women scorned are a formidable combination and Sherlock Holmes may have taken on more than he could handle. Their action would have been aimed at exposing him for what he was, and a complaint would have been lodged at Scotland Yard.

Eventually it would have come to Mycroft's ears. The scandal could be hushed up, certainly. Although there was the awkward fact of the cheque made out to Sherlock Holmes, that could be got over.

But enough was enough. No doubt Mycroft called round to Baker Street, perhaps taking Dr. Watson with him, and broke the news to his brother. The game up. Sherlock Holmes was finished.

The rest is history. In October of 1903 Sherlock Holmes retired to the Sussex Downs to keep bees. He was twice heard of again. In 1909 he solved the mystery of *The Lion's Mane* on the coast near his new home, writing the account himself, and in August, 1914, he played a major part in the arrest of the German spy Von Bork, near Harwich in Essex. Watson was present on that occasion, but again did not write the report.

Dr. Watson, after leaving Baker Street in the summer of 1902, took up his pen again to record more of the adventures of his old friend. His literary success was even greater than between the years of 1891 and 1904. After leaving Baker Street, his first step was to resurrect Holmes from the dead.

The public, after all, were still under the impression that Holmes's body lay at the foot of the Reichenhach Falls. In October, 1903, *The Strand Magazine* published *The Empty House*, revealing finally that Holmes was alive and well and re-established in Baker Street. Ironically, by this time he was living in retirement on the South Downs.

Between September, 1903, and January, 1905, thirteen Sherlock Holmes stories appeared in the *Strand*. Others followed at intervals until September, 1914, when the magazine began serialising *The Valley of Fear*. The stories were to continue until 5th March, 1907, when the last, *The Adventure of Shoscombe Old Place*, appeared.

Dr John H. Watson had published four novels and fifty-six short stories. He was never to write again. On Wednesday, 24th July, 1929, he was found at his apartment in Queen Anne Street by his housekeeper. He had died quietly in his sleep.

After 1914, Sherlock Holmes was never again heard of by the public. There is speculation that following his capture of the German agent Von Bork, he was involved in a secret wartime mission to Germany, from which he never returned. British Government documents which could confirm or refute this are still the subject of secrecy laws.

His death has never been recorded.

BIBLIOGRAPHY

Baring-Gould, William S.: Sherlock Holmes: a Biography. London, 1963
    The Chronological Holmes. New York, 1955
Begg, Paul: Jack the Ripper: the Uncensored Facts. London, 1989
Begg, Fido & Skinner: The Jack the Ripper A - Z. London, 1991
Doyle, Arthur Conan: A Study in Scarlet, 1887
    The Sign of the Four, 1889
    The Adventures of Sherlock Holmes, 1892
    The Memoirs of Sherlock Holmes, 1894
    The Hound of the Baskervilles, 1902
    The Return of Sherlock Holmes, 1905
    The Valley of Fear, 1915
    His Last Bow, 1917
    The Case-Book of Sherlock Holmes, 1927
Farmer, Philip José: Tarzan Alive. New York, 1972
Fido, Martin: The Crimes, Detection and Death of Jack the Ripper. London, 1972
Hardwick, Michael & Mollie: The Sherlock Holmes Companion. London, 1962
Harrison, Michael : In the Footsteps of Sherlock Holmes. London, 1971
    The World of Sherlock Holmes. London, 1973
Harrison, Paul: Jack the Ripper: the Mystery Solved. London, 1991
Holroyd, J.E. (ed): Seventeen Steps to 221B. London, 1965
McQueen, Ian: Sherlock Holmes Detected. London, 1974
Odell, Robin: Jack the Ripper in Fact and Fiction. London, 1965
Pointer, Michael: The Sherlock Holmes File. London, 1976
Roberts, S.C.: Holmes and Watson: A Miscellany. London, 1953
Rumbelow, Donald: The Complete Jack the Ripper. London, 1988
Tracy, Jack: Encyclopædia Sherlockiana. London, 1978
Utechin, Nicholas: Sherlock Holmes at Oxford. Oxford, 1977

APPENDIX

THE CRIMES OF SHERLOCK HOLMES

1887 May :	Blackmail of the King of Bohemia.
1888 January:	Burglary of Professor Moriarty's rooms.
August:	Murder of Mary Nichols.
September:	Murder of Mrs A. Chapman.
September:	Murder of Elizabeth Stride.
September:	Murder of Mrs C. Eddowes.
November:	Murder of M.J. Kelly
1889 June:	Conspiracy to pervert the course of Justice. Allowed an innocent man to stand trial for murder and the guilty man to go free.
1890 December:	Fraud. He defrauded his client in *The Beryl Coronet* of £3,000.
1891 April:	Murder of Professor Moriarty.
1894 April:	Murder of the Hon. Ronald Adair.
April:	Conspiracy to prervert the course of justice. He attempted to frame Colonel Sebastian Moran for the Adair murder.
1897 January:	Accessory in the murder of Sir Eustace Brackenstall.
March:	Accessory in the murder of Mortimer Tregennis
1899 January:	Burglary of Charles Augustus Milverton's premises.
January:	Accessory to the murder of Milverton and destruction of material evidence.
1901 May:	Conspiracy to pervert the course of justice; aiding a kidnapper and withholding material evidence in the affair at the Priory School.
1903 May:	Blackmail of Isadora Klein

INDEX

Abbey Grange 46,149,153,163
Adair, Ronald 137,172
Adams, Constance 5,82
Adler, Felix 5
Adler, Irene 5,93,129
Agar, Moore 156
Amberley, Josiah 149,160
Anderson, Robert 74,86
Armstrong, Leslie 151
Backwater, Lord 38,40
Baker Street Irregulars 41,46
Baldwin, Ted 55
Baring-Gould, William 3, 5, 19, 97, 129
Baritsu 88,112
Baynes, Inspector 96
Bell, Joseph 134
Bellinger, Lord 40
Bellord Domestic Agency 94
Beryl Coronet 15,106,108
Bexhill Convalescent Home 78
Black Peter 88,149,152
Blanched Soldier 171
Blue Carbuncle 37,53
Bohemia, King of 5,172
Boscombe Valley Mystery 38,96
Brackenstall, Eustace 153
Brackwell, Eva 161
Brookfield, Charles 135
Bruce-Partington Plans 18, 42, 149
Burnet, Miss 102
Burnwell, George 15
Cardboard Box 38,98
Carfax, Frances 41,169,171
Carroll, Lewis 25
Case of Identity 14,37,52,132
Chapman, Annie 71,85
Charles Augustus Milverton 163
Clarence, Duke of 72
Clay, John 38,52,57
Copper Beeches 38,94,96
Creeping Man 169,175
Croker, Captain 155

Crooked Man 38,98
Cubitt, Hilton 150,160
Cutbush, Thomas 73
Damery, James 170
Dancing Men 160
De Quincy, Thomas 25
De Merville, Violet 170,171
Devil's Foot 81,150,159
Dew, Walter 88
Disappearance of Lady Frances Carfax 41
Dixie, Steve 172
Dodgson, Charles L 25
Douglas, John 55
Dovercourt, Earl of 161
Doyle, Arthur Conan 133,148,168
Druitt, Montague 73
Dunbar, Grace 164
Dying Detective 37,53,82,148
Eddowes, Catherine 71,85
Ellgin-Johnson, Chris 83
Empty House 88, 116, 132, 139, 147, 177
Engineer's Thumb 38,98,108
Ernest, Ray 160
Farquhar, Mr 108
Ferguson, Robert 153
Fido, Martin 79
Final Problem 90,108,118,144
Five Orange Pips 37, 49, 64, 88, 112
Forrester, Mrs Cecil 65
Fraser, James 74
Garcia, Aloysius 98
Gibson, J Neil 164
Gloria Scott 18,27,43,112
Golden Pince-Nez 149,152
Greek Interpreter 18, 20, 38, 81, 84, 91, 103
Gregson, Tobias 36, 45, 84, 98, 170
Greuze, Jean B 59
Gruner, Baron 170
Gull, William 72
Hamund, St John 135

Harding, John V 155
Harrison, Michael 27
Hayes, Reuben 166
Henderson, Mr 102
Hicks, Seymour 135
His Last Bow 88,145
Holder, Alexander 15
Holder, Arthur 15
Holdernesse, Duke of 32,165
Holmes, Mycroft 18, 42, 126, 130, 145, 151, 152
Holmes, Sherrrinford 20,34
Holmes, Siger 20
Holmes, Violet 21
Holmes, Mrs. 27
Hope, Trelawney 40
Hopkins, Stanley 46,149,152
Hound of the Baskervilles 38, 81, 84,136,168
Hudson, Morse 43
Hudson, Mrs 14,43,82,131
Huxtable, Thorneycroft 32,165
Illustrious Client 42,170
Jack the Ripper 3,70
Johnson, Shinwell 42
Jones, Athelney 65,84,111
Jones, Peter 52
Kelly, Mary J 71,94
Kensington 5,82,131
Klein, Isadora 172
Knight, Stephen 72
Kosminski, Aaron 74
Ku Klux Klan 49
Langham Hotel 14
Lawende, Joseph 79
Leather Apron 87
Lestrade, Sholto 36, 40, 45, 140, 152, 162
Lion's Mane 175
Long, Elizabeth 79
Lucas, Mr 102
Lusk, George 86
Maberley, Mary 172
MacDonald, Inspector 38,57,126
MacFarlane, John H 149,152
Macnaghten, Melville 73,86
Man with the Twisted Lip 37,48
Mason, White 61

Maupertius, Baron 38,47
Mazarin Stone 175
Milverton, Charles A 160
Missing Threequarter 94,149,151
Montague Street 19,26,29
Montpelier 21,131
Moran, Augustus 116
Moran, Sebastian 116,129,137
Morcar, Countess of 53
Moriarty, James 3, 42, 56, 108, 172
Morstan, Mary 65, 82, 97, 108, 151, 168
Munro, Grant 84
Munro, James 74
Murillo, Don 104
Musgrave, Reginald 18,29
Musgrave Ritual 18,29
Naval Treaty 38,92,97
Netley, John 72
Newnes, George 132
Nichols, Mary A 70
Noble Bachelor 37,40
Norton, Godfrey 7,129
Norwood Builder 149,175
Openshaw, John 49,83,109
Ostrog, Michael 74
Overton, Cyril 149
Oxford University 22,25
Packer, Matthew 89
Patterson, Inspector 126
Phelps, Percy 92,97
Pike, Langdale, 41
Porlock, Fred 42,55,111
Prendergast, Major 90
Presbury, Professor 175
Priory School 32,165
Pycroft, Hall 97
Rance, John 46
Randall family 154
Red Headed League 37, 52, 57, 111, 132
Red Circle 170,175
Reigate Squires 37,47
Resident Patient 37,39
Retired Colourman 149,160
Rogers, Charles 135,145
Ronder, Mrs 150,152

Saltire, Lord 166
Sandeford, Mr 163
Savage, Victor 38,53
Scandal in Bohemia 5, 37, 48, 52, 132, 172
Scandinavia, King of 11,38
Scott-Eccles, John 36,98
Scowrers 55
Second Stain 37,40,43
Sherlock Holmes 135
Sherlock Holmes Baffled 147
Sherman, Old 23
Sherrinford, Edward 21
Shoshcombe Old Place 135, 169, 177
Sickert, Joseph 72
Sickert, Walter 72
Sign of Four 38, 81, 84, 92, 132, 151, 168
Silver Blaze 106,108
Six Napoleons 45,163
Smith, Culverton, 53
Smith, Henry 74
Smith, Violet 152
Smith, William 79
Smith, Willoughby 152
Solitary Cyclist 88,150,152
Speckled Band 37,39
St Bartholomew's Hospital 28, 35, 92
St Clair, Neville 49
St Simon, Robert 40
Stamford, Dr 133
Sterndale, Leon 159
Stockbroker's Clerk 38,97,108
Stoner, Helen 39
Stowell, Thomas 72
Straker, John 106

Stride, Elizabeth 71,85
Study in Scarlet 18, 23, 35, 37, 45, 64,82,88,112,132,168
Sussex Vampire 149,152
Swanson, Donald 76
Tabram, Martha 93
Thor Bridge 164
Three Gables 172
Three Garridebs 41,168
Three Students 87,149
Tregennis, Brenda 159
Tregennis, Mortimer 159
Trevelyan, Percy 39
Trevor, Victor 27,29,43
Turner, Martha 11,93
Under the Clock 135
Utechin, Nicholas 23
Valley of Fear 38, 42, 55, 70, 92, 109, 177
Veiled Lodger 150,152
Vermissa Valley 55
Verner, Dr 151
Von Bork, - 177
Von Herder, - 142
Von Kramm, Count 5
Warner, John 103
Warren, Charles 74,86
White, Stephen 78,86,91
Whitney, Elias 48
Whitney, Isa 48
Whitney, Kate 48
Wilder, James 166
Wilson, Colin 92
Winter, Kitty 170
Wisteria Lodge 36,96
Wolfe, Nero 129
Wright, E Barton 112
Yellow Face 38,84,112

The photographs in this book are from the author's collection and also from the collections of Victoria and Kate Mitchelson and of Pamela Wilkes.